Llanfair Cly

History of a Cardiganshire Parish

Alan Leech

Published by the author

Aerial view above, © Crown copyright: Royal Commission on the Ancient and Historical Monuments of Wales

Aerial view of the parish of Llanfair Clydogau and view of St. Mary's Church showing bell tower.

Copyright © Alan Leech

Published in 2008 by
Alan Leech
Tan yr esgair
Llanfair Clydogau
Ceredigion
SA48 8LJ

The right of Alan Leech to be identified as the author of the work has been asserted by him in accordance with the Copyright, Designs and Patents Act 1988

All rights reserved. No part of this publication may be reproduced, stored in a retrieval system, or transmitted, in any form or by any means, electronic, mechanical, photocopying, recording or otherwise, without the prior written permission of the publisher.

ISBN 978-0-9561116-0-9

Printed and bound by:

Gwasg Gomer Cyfyngedig,
Llandysul, Ceredigion.

Dedicated to my father, Tom Leech, an inspirational local historian who also encouraged tolerance, curiosity and a spirit of optimism.

Contents	Page
Preface	
Chapter One: Introduction	1 - 12
• Religious worship and the parish	2
• The environment of Llanfair Clydogau	3
• Early history of the Llanfair Clydogau area	6
• Early history of the church	7
• Plas Llanfair	11
Chapter Two: The parish between 1500 and 1599	13 - 17
Chapter Three: The parish between 1600 and 1699	18 - 24
Chapter Four: The parish between 1700 and 1799	25 - 40
• Church records of baptisms, marriages and burials	29
• Burial and interment within the church	29
• Llanfair Mansion (Plas Llanfair)	30
• Lead and silver mining	32
• The poor of the parish	37

Contents

	Page
• Llanfair crime	38
• Llanfair freeholders and leaseholders in 1760	39
• The Llanfair Clydogau Estate of Thomas Johnes of Havod in 1791	40

Chapter Five: The parish between 1800 and 1899 — 41 - 133

	Page
• Llanfair crime	43
• Sale of the Llanfair Demesne	44
• The "arrival" of Lord Carrington	46
• The economy of Llanfair	47
• Health and the standard of living	49
• The growth, then decline of the population of Llanfair	49
• Llanfair population statistics 1801-1901	50
• Llanfair occupations	54
• Lead and silver mining	55

Contents

	Page
• Jonathan Marsden of Llanfair Mines	64
• Manufacturing and grain processing on the Llanfair Road	67
• Shops and retail activities	71
• Education in the Llanfair area	71
• Llanfair School	78
• 1881 Aberdare Report on Education	83
• Llanfair Evening Continuation School	84
• Daniel Jenkins: Llanfair School "teacher in charge" or headteacher	85
• John Thomas: famous photographer	85
• Church records	85
• Burial records	86
• Capel Mair	86
• 1836 Tithe Commutation Act	91

Contents   **Page**

- Llanfair Clydogau Parish, tithe details of 16th October 1839 — 91 - 102
- Religious Census of 1851 — 102
- The gaoling of the vicar and his "visitation of God" — 104
- Morgan Williams: early years and appointment to Llanfair — 106
- Morgan Williams: his business and financial activities — 109
- Morgan Williams: his personal and family circumstances — 112
- Morgan Williams: dealing with his imprisonment — 114
- The scramble to appoint a vicar in 1859/1860 — 119
- The power of Lord Carrington — 121
- 1860 the Glebe — 122
- Development of the railway — 123
- Lord Carrington's sale of lands — 124

Contents

	Page
• Purchase of Llanfair lands by William Jones of Glandenys	124
• Rebuilding of St Mary's Church	125
• Parish poor and the Poor Law	128
• Sunday Schools	130
• Servants and farming in the 19th century	133

Chapter Six: The parish between 1900 and 2008 — 134 - 220

- Llanfair population statistics — 135
- Llanfair School — 137
- The Value Office Survey, 1910-15 — 148 - 152
- The Llanfair economy in 1910 — 153
- The Poor Law — 154
- First World War (1914-18) — 155
- First World War Roll of Honour — 158

Contents

	Page
• Parish tragedies in the early 19th century	160
• Llanfair Agricultural Show	161
• The graves near "the hill of the holy place"	168
• 1920's the Glebe land	171
• The Women's Institute	172
• Sale of the Glandenys Estate in 1930	175
• Sale of the Derry Ormond Estate in 1944	176
• Second World War (1939-45)	177
• Llanfair Clydogau Welcome Home Fund	179
• Parish Memorial Fund for Second World War dead	182
• Cardiganshire Home Guard	182
• Evacuees from the city	184
• The 1941-3 Government Farm Survey	185
• Derelict Llanfair farms	189

Contents

	Page
• An alternative lifestyle: inward migration	192
• Sunday Schools	193
• The church and the parish	196
• The parish graveyard	198
• Visiting the graves of ancestors	200
• Displays of remembrance within the church	200
• Church Hall	201
• Maintaining the church and graveyard	205
• The Llanfair and Cellan Young Farmers Club (YFC)	206
• Forestry Commission	209
• Longwood	210
• Shops	211
• Snippets of news from Llanfair	212

Contents   Page

- Capel Mair   214
- Llanfair History Exhibition: August 2008   217
- Some Llanfair residents   218
- Conclusion   220

Appendices   221 - 232

- Appendix One: Vicars of St. Mary's   221
- Appendix Two: Ministers of Capel Mair   222
- Appendix Three: Elders of Capel Mair   223
- Appendix Four: High Sheriffs of Cardiganshire from Plas Llanfair and Members of Parliament from Plas Llanfair or Hafod   224
- Appendix Five: References   225 - 232

Preface

Llanfair Clydogau is a parish within the Teifi Valley in West Wales. It currently has a population of about 240 persons and just over 100 occupied houses and farms, spread over approximately 4,500 acres of predominantly upland, on the edge of the Cambrian Mountains. Its scattered farms and houses straddle both sides of the major, north east to south west flowing River Teifi, and its east bank tributary, the River Clywedog. The parish occupies land up to about 1,400 feet in height. Its position as a civil parish ended in May 1987 when it was joined as a community council with the nearby parish of Cellan.

The community is very mixed with both Welsh and English speakers. The former tend to be from the main farming families of the area, some of whom have roots going back several hundred years. The latter have come to live in the parish, mainly during the last 30 years, from England. They have tended to purchase houses and small holdings made available by the movement away of the local people, probably for economic reasons. In 2000 the per capita income was below 75% of the European average. The inward migrants tend to be seeking an alternative to life elsewhere, often the south east of England. There is a fine community spirit and the parish possesses a shop, containing a Post Office and both a church and chapel.

It is an area of much beauty, history and tranquillity. It is attractive to holiday makers seeking rural peace, and a number of the local farms or small holdings offer self catering or bed and breakfast accommodation for visitors.

My wife Sally and I bought a former small holding here in 1998 and after seeing the building renovated, moved to the parish in 1999 from Hampshire. Since then we have participated in its life and work and feel very much at home here. Through my attendance at services held at St Mary's, I began to learn something of the history of the church within the area. Hence, when someone pointed out that there was no publication outlining the history of

Llanfair, I decided to try to research the subject and began to collect information, documents and photographs. I have sought to locate all written accounts about the parish and used them as a basis for this history.

I thank Sally for her support and tolerance of the time I have spent in visiting Aberystwyth's National Library of Wales, Ceredigion Archives, Carmarthenshire Archives, the National Archives and the Lampeter University Library, and for her help in checking through my writings. I am grateful to her also for her skill in producing the maps within this publication, her cover design, and for editorial work. I am grateful to the following local residents for letting me copy and use photographs and documents which they hold: Iris Quan; Gwyneth Jones; Tim Evans; Arwyn Evans; Ian Evans; Deborah and David Jones; Arwyn and Eleri Davies; Aneurin Davies; Odwyn Davies; Laura Wood; Elizabeth Mercer; Lesley Stevens; Evan Davies; Beti and John Davies; Tom Thomas; Caroline Pilcher; Isobel Taylor; Aerwen and Dan Griffiths; Ieuan Thomas; Robert Grey; Alun Jenkins; Noel of Beulah; Anna Rummey and Dave Clarke. I am sorry if I have failed to mention someone who has given me information. For ease of understanding I have referred to the county by the name Cardiganshire, rather than the current local authority description of Ceredigion.

Consistency with the spelling of place names is a problem, since many words have changed over time. In order to deal with this, when quoting from a historic document or map I have used the spelling shown, but when referring to a property or place at the present time, I have used the currently accepted form of its spelling.

I have done my best to check the accuracy of all my sources, documents I have utilised and also to list references. If there are inaccuracies or deficiencies in descriptions and conclusions drawn, then responsibility resides with me.

Alan Leech,
November 2008.

Introduction

The meaning of Llanfair Clydogau is village or church (llan) of Mary (Mair, which in usage mutates to "fair",) on the banks of the three Clywedog streams called the Clywedog Uchaf, Clywedog Ganol and Clywedog Isaf. These flow off the western edge of the lower slopes of the Cambrian Mountains on the Cardiganshire - Carmarthenshire border, in a south westerly direction and soon after, uniting together, become the River Clywedog, before entering the River Teifi. The three streams are collectively called Clywedogau or Clydogau. It is within the area adjacent to the Clywedog, just on the eastern edge of the Teifi's flood plain, that the oldest known buildings within the parish are located. Here, St Mary's Church was built, as was the historic manor house of Plas Llanfair. This location was also a central point for the communications network. It was the meeting place of the north-south road from Llanddewi Brefi to Cellan, the west-east road from Lampeter and Llangybi, the former Roman road of Sarn Helen and tracks leading onto the eastern uplands of the Cambrian Mountains.

This site of the oldest development is where the main valley (Teifi) is about a ½ mile wide, at a height of approximately 400 feet, with a reasonable amount of fairly flat land between the river itself and the edge of the river plain. The lower land gives way to the steeper slopes leading to higher ground, on the east to the mountains drained by the Clywedog and on the west, to the upland ridge which divides the parish from that nearby in Llangybi. This location is slightly above the main part of the flood plain of the Teifi. At this site, was built the church for Llanfair and the manor house, with the parish spread out on both sides of the River Teifi for a short distance along the river to the north and south, and up on the steeper and higher land to both sides of the valley.

In seeking to understand and explain the history of the parish one needs firstly, to understand the origin and history of the church, since the parish as a unit of administration, was established in conjunction and in association with it.

Chapter One   Introduction

Religious worship and the parish

Written records of either the church or parish are few in number before the 16th century, and hence it is extremely difficult to date the foundation of the parish, the church or the Llanfair manor house, (Plas Llanfair), by precise documentary means. However, it is clear that the church occupied a pivotal

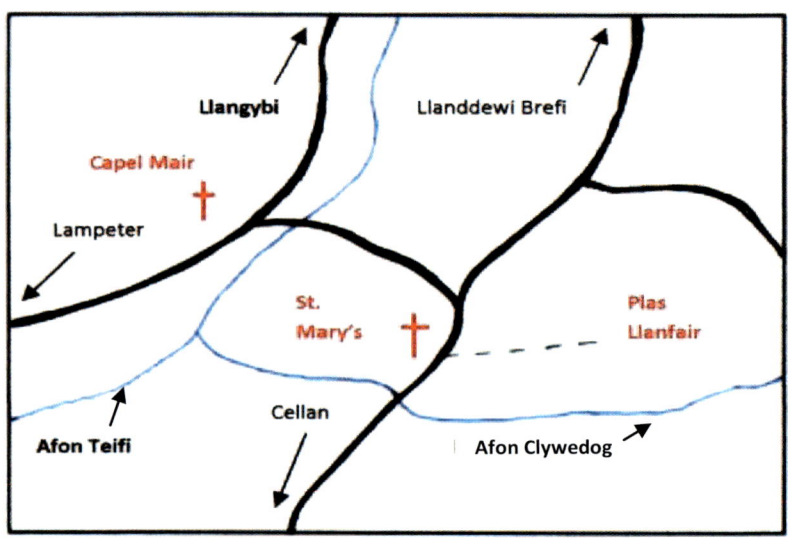

Llanfair Parish : St. Mary's Church, Capel Mair and Plas Llanfair

(not drawn to scale)

role within the community throughout most of recent history, and that a study of the development and life of the church is in many ways, a study of the evolution and life of the parish, not only as a religious, but also as a secular entity. For instance, we can track the generality of the parish population through church records of baptism, marriage and burial. These same records allow us to study the spread of population away from the valley bottom adjacent to the River Teifi, on to the lower, and later middle slopes of the three Clywedog streams, and to seek to understand changes in the local economy. A study of the church also gives us an insight into the nature of the local society, with its hierarchy ranging from those rich and powerful men who gave to themselves the title Esq., who owned much land and had a steady and reliable income plus a large house, to those who were described as paupers, and who possessed no assets and had no income. Few of the important events within the parish have taken place without the church having some role within them. However, from 1790, the religious situation in the parish began to change, with the development of an alternative centre of worship. This non conformist Christian worship was from 1825, located at the Independent Capel Mair. Both church and chapel share the same parish graveyard, and for a number of years, only the church could be used as a centre for baptism, marriage and burial. Hence the importance of the church records in respect to these important family events within the parish.

The environment of Llanfair Clydogau.

The main characteristic of the environment which has shaped the human and economic development of the parish is its climate and the nature of the local soils. That is because the principal pattern, location and growth of population was largely based upon agriculture, and the main determinant of the type, scale and richness of agriculture, is the climate, combined with nature of soil composition and underlying rock structures. Climatically, the most significant feature is the relatively high levels of rainfall of more than 40 inches per annum on the lowest land, rising to over 60 inches on the mountain slopes which rise to a height of over 1500 feet to the east, beyond the county boundary with Carmarthenshire. An approximate indication of the local weather information is provided by the Meteorological Station at Trawscoed, about 20 miles to the north, which records an annual rainfall average of 47 inches for its site, and the number of rainfall days as, on average, 169, per year. As a comparative indicator of the degree of

Chapter One   Introduction

wetness for the Cardiganshire area, Ross on Wye on the Wales/Herefordshire border, experiences an average of only 27 inches of rain with only 114 rainfall days.

In eastern Cardiganshire, as a result of the high local rainfall, soils are frequently wet and acidic and pastoral farming was, and still is, the main economic activity, with much of the higher land described as rough pasture, only able to be successfully farmed by sheep. The river valley of the Teifi possesses deposits of fertile water borne alluvium, on which the larger and more affluent farms are located. These farms largely have elements of this lower land, linked to some higher land pastures. Most of the main economically vibrant farming is located below the 700 foot contour line. Farming on the lower river valley lands is more able to sustain cattle, and it is here, that those mixed farms with an emphasis upon dairy farming developed in the 19th and 20th century. Some of these survive today. Across the parish, the main emphasis historically, was upon animal rearing for sale as food to English markets. These animals were collected and then moved out from Cardiganshire along drovers' routes across the mountains. Some Llanfair men described their occupation as "drover" in the 19th century census returns.

The contrast between the lower and higher lands is an important one in terms of the history of development, subsequent settlement and later depopulation of the parish. The higher land away from the valley has thinner, coarser soil, on slopes which receive a great deal of rainfall. Farming here was, and still is where it survives, concentrated very much upon sheep rearing.

The other factor which has affected population location, distribution, and both its growth and subsequent decline, is the availability of raw materials for mining and manufacturing. Beds of lead ore, with silver, were found in the 1750's adjacent to the River Clywedog. This discovery caused a mini building boom which saw mine shafts sunk and the construction of houses close to what was then, the Llanfair Manor house. Some writers suggest that it was the closeness of this development which made the then owner of

Chapter One   Introduction

___

the house, Thomas Johnes, less enthusiastic about living there, an action which helped to contribute to the demise of the building, its subsequent collapse and eventual disappearance. Though the mines ceased production in the middle years of the 19th century, most of the associated houses, commercial premises and offices remain in the vicinity of Silvermine Cottage, and are today occupied as homes. The mine shafts have largely been filled in.

The other significant local raw material was wool. On the basis of a good supply from the local sheep, along with a ready supply of water for washing and water power, a local woollen industry developed in the 19th century, along the Llanfair Road in the vicinity of Pandy and Llanfair Mill. The latter was already making use of this water power for grinding corn when the woollen industry began to develop in the middle years of the 19th century. This woollen industry had ceased by about 1930. To accompany this manufacturing development, a number of houses and a small factory were built. Most of these buildings have survived and exist today as homes.

View of Teifi valley showing Llanfair Clydogau, looking south west

Bryn Cysegrfan from the east

Chapter One — Introduction

Early history of the Llanfair Clydogau area.

The earliest evidence of settled human activity in the area goes back a long way in history. With the Roman occupation of Britain, the military power constructed a series of forts and roads in Wales. One, Sarn Helen, ran from LLanio in Cardiganshire, to the station at Llanfair ar y Bryn in Carmarthenshire. Its characteristic straightness can be seen today as it climbs the eastern side of the Teifi valley between Llanfair and Ffarmers in Carmarthenshire.

The Ordnance Survey map shows, on the slopes of Bryn Cysegrfan to the east of the River Teifi, a symbol which is used to denote a place of considerable antiquity. The Vicar, Jonathan Evans[1], writing in 1909, calls the hill Bryn Cyser Fan (the hill of the holy place), and says local tradition has it that the long barrows here are graves. An account of the site written by Trevor Lewis[2] of Aberystwyth University in 1927, refers to the hill as Bryn Cysegrfan (hill sacred spot) and describes the hillside as containing twenty two "graves". "They are rectangular in shape surrounded by a shallow depression, but stand up from the ground as distinctive mounds". He points out that during 1927, archaeological investigations took place on the Bryn Cysegrfan "graves", but that nothing was found inside them. He goes on to describe 28 of these long mounds, four round ones, one with an L shape and one in the shape of a cross. He states that "in our survey we noticed that several had been cut into, either out of curiosity, or to obtain stone". "All correspond in that they were erected by scooping up the mound from the depression around them. The natural turf is intact in each case, and above it, the heaped up stones and soil form the mound. It appears that the builders of these structures took one or more of the natural boulders as nuclei, and in some cases piled up a heap of stones which they covered with a layer of soil". Precisely what the mounds were was inconclusive at this point. However, further archaeological work was undertaken in 1978 and 1979, and an account was written by David Austin[3] of Lampeter University. He pointed out that on the hillside of Bryn Cysegrfan were four

Chapter One — Introduction

rectangular structures or buildings and 36 pillow mounds. He stated that he believes the pillow mounds were used for rabbit farming, "the rabbit was an expensive delicacy of the lord's table". Radio carbon dating of vegetation associated with one mound suggested an origin of about AD 1315-1415.The research led him to suggest that one or more of the stone buildings was associated with supervision of the warren. He said that other of the structures may just have been used for seasonal residence associated with the grazing of sheep on summer upland pastures or hafod, but there is no specific dating suggested for these, except that they are likely to be more recent than the mounds.

Early history of the church

The St Mary's church building as we see it today is not the original. It appears to have been rebuilt or remodelled several times, with the latest occurring between 1885-8[4], to a design by Middletown, Prothero and Philpott. It used a shell which had apparently been previously remodelled in the 1840's.

We have no clear written record of the church before 1535 when there is a reference in the *Valor Ecclesiasticus*[5] of Henry VIII. Determining a precise date for its origin is impossible. Lewis[6] in 1825 described it as small and ancient. Another refers to the original building as dating from the 15th century. Several pointers exist to suggest a church foundation from earlier than 1535. Firstly, the very old yew tree in the church yard might well afford some indication of the length of human activity on the site. The tree's girth is 693 cm, which makes it one of the largest in Cardiganshire. A writer in the Cardiganshire County History[7], estimates that a yew with a girth of 700 cm may be approximately 750 years old. If this calculation is correct, then it would suggest activity at the St Mary's site in the 1200's. Secondly, close by it is known that there was settled and, relatively rich economic human activity from an early date , in that there was a significant and very important manor house. This was owned and occupied by one of the richest and most politically powerful families in West Wales. Located

Chapter One — Introduction

some 200 yards away from the church (just beyond Llanfair Fawr), this mansion, Plas Llanfair Clywedogau, existed until the late 18th century when, following a period of neglect by the owners, it became a ruin of which nothing today remains. Plas Llanfair was known as a magnificent residence which had an important part to play in both the social and political life of the area and indeed, the country at various times. Lewis in his 1825 account, describes the mansion as " a building of very great antiquity: the walls were in some places five yards in thickness, and in several parts of the building there was the date 1080". Yet he does not cite evidence for his belief in the accuracy of this date. We have no documentary evidence of the date of its foundation. Thirdly, the Royal Commission on the Ancient and Historical Monuments of Wales[8] express the view on their web site that the aerial photography they have of the church and its site, is suggestive of a very early foundation. Fourthly, the font within the church has been dated at about the 12th century. The font has recognisable symbols of the Evangelists carved from its stone. It is a square bowl with the symbols at the corners. Describing the font in 1913, a writer felt the bowl was of a late Norman date. "The man (a face only), the ox and the lion are conventional in form and rude in execution, especially is this so in the case of the lion that would not be so recognisable as such were it not for his companion figures. The eagle of St John however, is a fine bird in bold relief, and in a better state of preservation than the other emblems represented."[9]. The font is located at the rear of the church, set up on a brick plinth which aesthetically does not suit either the font itself or its location within the building. Clearly the plinth was constructed at some point in time unrelated to the rebuilding of the church in 1888.

The four evangelists were Matthew, Mark, Luke and John, whose names are attached to the New Testament Gospels. They are identified with the four living creatures described in Revelations. The link is as follows:

Chapter One Introduction

    Matthew   :   a human, a figure of humanity and reason;
    Mark   :   a lion, a figure of courage and monarchy;
    Luke   :   an ox, a figure of sacrifice, service and strength;
    John   :   an eagle, a figure of the sky.

The figures are shown with, or instead of the Evangelist in early medieval Gospel books. They are one of the most common motifs in early church locations. Similar fonts showing the Evangelists are located in the church at Maestir and Silian as well as that at Llanfair Clydogau. From the early 13th century their use began to decline as a new concept of Christ in Majesty, showing the wounds of the passion began to take over. Hence, the nature of the carvings on the font enables its dating.

Llanfair Church font

Chapter One   Introduction

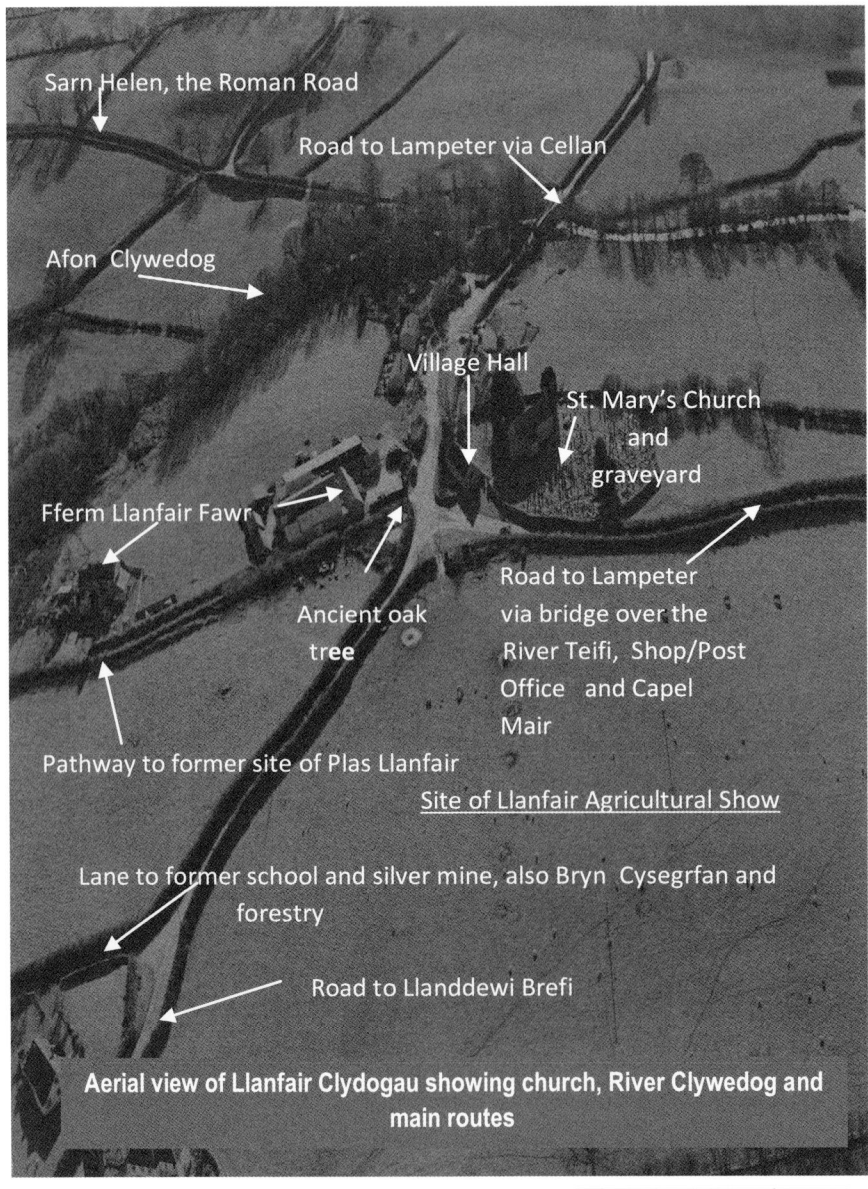

Aerial view of Llanfair Clydogau showing church, River Clywedog and main routes

Aerial view above, © Crown copyright: Royal Commission on the Ancient and Historical Monuments of Wales

For the above reasons it seems apparent that an early church existed on the St Mary's site. It would have been created at a time of much social, political and military upheaval in the years immediately following the Norman invasion of Britain in 1066. Conquests within the West Wales area were made, castles were built and conflict occurred between powerful invaders and alliances of the Welsh nobility. In 1282 King Edward united Wales with England by the Statutes of Rhuddlan and constituted Ceredigion into a county, by name Cardigan.

Plas Llanfair

According to Francis Jones[10,] the earliest reference to the manor house is in 1550 when David ap Evan Lloyd Vychan became High Sheriff of the County. The house remained in the Lloyd family until passing to Thomas Johnes of Dolaucothi in Carmarthenshire in the late 17th century. It subsequently passed to his cousin Thomas Johnes of Penybont,

Building remains believed to be Plas Llanfair in the garden of Clywedog Cottage (August 2008)

Tregaron, in 1734, and then to his son, also called Thomas Johnes, who, upon his marriage to an heiress, moved away to Castle Croft, Herefordshire. Before he left he was, in 1740, appointed a magistrate. In 1760, in a list of Cardiganshire freeholders[11], he is still named as holding lands at Llanfair, but his address is shown as Ludlow in Shropshire. He was the father of the more famous Thomas Johnes of Hafod, near Devil's Bridge. It is believed that in the late 18th century, Plas Llanfair was dismantled of personal belongings and left empty. Elizabeth Inglis-Jones[12] thinks it stood empty and crumbling for years before it fell down. We have written confirmation from Meyrick[13] that it was in ruins when he visited Llanfair Clydogau in the first decade of the 19th century. Another 19th century account of the site comes from Thomas Griffiths of Blaencwm, written about 1888/1890. He said "the site of this mansion was where Office Fawr's garden now is, so close to the river in which the servants did all the washing"[14]. Evidence to support this is provided by the photograph of the remains of the foundations of a building in the garden of what was once called Office Fawr, but is today a house called Clywedog Cottage.

It is clear that whoever owned the manor house, was also the predominant landowner within the parish. Many holdings of land belonged to the family living there and were occupied by tenants. Fortunately, some of the detail dealing with the legal transfers of some of these lands has survived in estate papers of some of the Cardiganshire gentry families, such as the Lloyds, Vaughans and Johnes. Where references have been found within these documents, they are quoted in the chapters which follow. They provide for us, not only an interesting though incomplete picture of the location of wealth and power, but also information on aspects of the religious, political, economic and social life of the time in Llanfair and also in Cardiganshire in general.

Chapter Two 1500 to 1599

The parish between 1500 and 1599

> Henry VII (1485-1509), Henry VIII (1509-1547), Edward VI (1547-1553), Mary I (1553-1558), Elizabeth I (1558-1603).
>
> **Significant developments**
>
> 1535 Pope excommunicated Henry VIII; 1536 and 1546 Acts of Union, Wales legally linked to England, land divided into shires, English became the official language; 1536 Parliament passed Act for the Dissolution of the Monasteries; 1537 first complete English translation of Bible, 1554 England formally rejoins Roman Catholic Church; 1559 re-establishment of protestant Church of England; 1588 Bible published in Welsh; late 16th century writings of William Shakespeare.

Various pieces of information allow us to know that there was a well established settlement and a social order in Llanfair in the 16th century. Yet, written evidence is in short supply. To understand why, it needs to be borne in mind that the population of Britain before the 16th century was very small in number, (it is estimated that Wales had a total population of about 270,000 at this time), and very few people were able to read and write, a situation which was not improved until the 19th century. Also, why would they have written, to whom, and where would anything recorded be kept? Writings about Cardiganshire up to this century were largely in Latin and principally related to the work of St David's diocese in structuring and administrating the Church, or were legal documents dealing with a will or a dispute. Later, by the 16th century, there was a growing use of English in legal documents such as wills and marriage settlements. All such documents that I have seen for this research mentioning Llanfair, were written in English.

Chapter Two 1500 to 1599

An interesting feature in interpreting the limited early documentation relating to what was a remote, very sparsely populated and relatively inaccessible area is the lack of a universal agreed way in which to spell various local place names. For instance Llanfair Cledogee, Fair Clvdoge, Llanuaiercledoye, Llanwayre Cledogre, and Llanvair Cledogre all appear as names for the parish in 16th century legal documents. The present spelling of the parish first appears in papers relating to local large land estates at the end of the 1780's and 1790's. The spelling used within the original documents has been retained below for all buildings, farms and parishes.

In relation to the 16th century, there is no specific written account of the size and nature of the church, or the parish in general. The church was a Catholic foundation linked to the collegiate church at Llanddewi Brefi. The Bible which was read was in Latin. An English and later Welsh translation, first appeared in this century, but it would have taken some time to attain a wide currency of use across the country.

The earliest written reference to St Mary's church was in the *Valor Ecclesiasticus of 1535*[1]. This large, six volume document written in Latin, was produced by commissioners acting for Henry VIII after he had taken over the English and Welsh Church in 1534. It was a systematic valuation of all ecclesiastical assets throughout England and Wales. The survey was carried out over a period of nine months and was available for use in 1536. The Llanfair Clydogau church (called Llanvair Cledogee) was referred to as being part of the collegiate church of Llanddewi Brefi, some four miles to the north. We know that Llanddewi was reconstituted as a collegiate church by Bishop Bek of St David's in 1287. In fact, it was during the 13th century that the diocesan ecclesiastical administration of a parish structure that still exists today was created. That is probably the time when the parish of Llanfair was formed. Over 200 years later, at the time of the *Valor Ecclesiasticus* of 1535, in the Deanery of Sub-Aeron, Thomas Lloyd, precentor of St David's, is shown as holding five out of the deanery's 30 benefices (church stipends), including Llanddewi and Llanfair. This was an unsatisfactory state of affairs. The writer Glanmor Williams[2] has concluded :

Chapter Two   1500 to 1599

"it would seem that about half of the benefices, including nearly all the more valuable ones, were in the hands of absentee incumbents who delegated the care of souls to poor beneficed clergy of the neighbourhood, or more usually, to unbeneficed stipendiary priests."

Following the takeover of the Catholic Church by the King, major changes occurred in its organisational structure across the country. In addition, the monasteries were dissolved in the 1540's. That would have had a great impact on this general area of Cardiganshire. This is because the operation and structure of the large Cistercian Abbey, with its enormous land estates at Strata Florida, Pontrhydfendigaid to the north of Tregaron, was destroyed and the land leased out and then sold off to rich landowners. As a result they became richer and more powerful. The ripple effect of this change would have reached out in all directions, affecting not only the operational structure of the Church within Cardiganshire, but also the management and structure of land ownership.

Apart from the *Valor Ecclesiasticus*, evidence of a developed society in the area, with some relatively affluent country or gentry families can be gained from heraldic records. For instance, research undertaken by *Lewis Dwnn*[3] in 1586, shows that Jenkyn Lloyd of Llanvair Klydoge married, in 1588, the daughter of John Stedman. Stedman was a very rich man who in 1571 had bought most of the Strata Florida lands. Jenkyn Lloyd, was the grandfather of Sir Walter Lloyd who was born in 1613, lived at the manor house of Plas Llanfair and became a member of parliament for Cardiganshire.

The will of Jenkin Lloyd of Llanvairclydoge of 1592 refers to him holding:

" seven messuages in Llanvairgledoge and of a mansion house in the same parish, with all its appurtenances, wherein the said Jenkin Lloyd during his lifetime lived"[4].

Messuages were houses and appurtances, land which went with them. Jenkin Lloyd was the main property and land owner at this time. He would have been a dominant force within the parish with links to the parish church.

Both his position within society and his link with the central position of the Church amongst the population, can be seen from an extract of his will. Upon his death he stipulated what should happen to his body and left a financial donation for the parish poor:

" First and principal I commend my soul unto Almighty God my maker and redeemer and my body to be buried in the parish church of Llanvair aforesaid.....I do give and bequeath to ye poor people of Llanvairgledogy forty shillings". (about £300 to £350 at today's values)

Another will of an important Llanfair resident concerns David ap Jevan[5] and dates from 1586. He stated:

"and my body to be buried in the parish church aforesaid".

He left 6s. 8d for the benefit of the poor of the parish.

A further example of the activities of rich landowners is shown in a Deed of the Crosswood Estate[6] of 1579, relating to "Letters Patent:

" being a grant in perpetuity to Sir Christopher Hatton, Knight of.... the collegiate church, the college and precentor of Llandewy Brevy, the site of the said college, the preband of Llanwayre Cledogoe and the right of the patronage, all in Co. Cardigan. The yearly rent for the property £40, the grantee to find the stipends of the incumbents".

The significance of this document is the transfer of ownership from the Vaughan family (Earls of Lisburne) who lived at Crosswood, of various church properties to Mr Hatton. He would collect a yearly rent and in exchange would be responsible for paying the salary of the priests at both Llanddewi Brefi and Llanfair Clydogau.

Another aspect of Llanfair of which we have knowledge was the importance of its leading families in the wider life of Cardiganshire. David ab

Chapter Two   1500 to 1599

Evan Llwyd Fychan was High Sheriff in 1551, 1557 and 1570. Jenkin Lloyd undertook the same role in 1578 and 1591.

Chapter Three 1600 to 1699

The parish between 1600 and 1699

Elizabeth I (to 1603), James I (1603-25), Charles I (1625-49), Charles II (1660-85), James II (1685-88), William III and Mary II (1689-1702).

Significant developments

1611 King James version of Bible; 1642 1st English Civil war; 1648 2nd English Civil War; 1648 Charles I beheaded; Commonwealth of England; 1655 Thomas Cromwell (Lord Protector) forbad Protestant services; 1701 seed drill invented-changes agriculture; Quakerism; 1665 Plague.

Several accounts give us a taste of life in Llanfair Clydogau in the 1600's, a period during which the population rose slowly. It was perhaps 350,000 in 1620 for the whole of Wales. Hence, the parish population was unlikely to exceed a few dozen people, or perhaps a hundred at its maximum by the end of the century.

One account is provided by documentation showing legal action being taken during the reign of James 1, involving Walter Lloyd of Llanfair Mansion[1]. Legal action was taken against him by a London merchant Robert Bowyer, concerning property and lands in the area. The written account of the court case alleges that Walter Lloyd agreed to buy property and land in Llanvairecledoge and LLandewbreve for £110 in 1617, but that he had refused to pay. Mr Lloyd asserted in court that he had made no such agreement to buy these properties.

Another land dispute during the reign of James 1 (1603-1625) concerned as plaintiffs, Symon Batten of Llanvayergledoge[2], described as a gent, and his wife Jane, and as defendants, John Griffith, Ellen Griffith, Lleyky Owen his sister, and Jevan Griffith Morgan. The dispute concerned a messuage and lands called Tythyn y Plas maes Clyewdoge and a messuage and lands called Tir yr hen velin in Llanvayergledoge.

Further information of the social fabric of the parish, as well as the orderly and settled nature of the population, is provided in the Cwrtmawr Deed[3] of 1613. This refers to: "grant from Thomas Lloyd of Llangynlli, county Cardigan, clerk to Evan ap Rees of Llanvair Cledoge, gent, and John Jones of Llanddewi Brevi, gent, of the capital messuage in which he resides, called Bronwydd".

One of the most nationally famous residents of Llanfair was the aforementioned Sir Walter Lloyd of Plas Llanfair. He was born in 1580 and reported as having matriculated from Lincoln College, Oxford at the age of 15 in November 1595. In 1615 he was admitted as a student of the Inner Temple, and six years later served as High Sheriff of Cardiganshire. He became the Member of Parliament for Cardiganshire, was made Commissioner of Array by Charles 1 in 1642 and knighted in 1643. He was a supporter of the monarchy in the First English Civil War, as were a large number of other landed gentry, and thus, as a punishment Parliament declared him "disabled to sit" in the House in 1643. A new writ for the Parliamentary constituency was issued and Sir Richard Pryse of Gogerddan was returned[4]. Various attempts were made to punish Walter Lloyd financially for his stance. In a letter from the Cardigan County Committee to the Committee for Compoundery in London in 1646, it was stated that: "father and son, John Lloyd and Walter Lloyd of Llanvair Clydogau; information that they are delinquent and unsequestrated". Other correspondence between the two Cardigan and London Committees took place in 1650. The correspondence referred to "Lloyd of Llanvair being summoned to answer a charge of delinquency laid against him by Lady Moore, acknowledging that during these troubles"(the Civil War), " he has lived on his Estates, which lay in the King's quarters and adhered to that party" (i.e. the King), " in the first War".

Earlier than this, he had in 1647, been fined £1,003.9s.0d for his behaviour and was again fined three years later, a further £261.10s.6d, owing to an error in identifying him as the same person who had been fined before[5]. These were large sums of money.

Sir Walter's family line, in terms of inheritance and the Llanfair estate, passed upon his death in about 1662, to his son Thomas, whose daughter Elizabeth married Thomas Johnes, Esq. of Dolaucothi, hence transferring Plas Llanfair and its lands to the Johnes branch of the family. The Llanfair estates were firmly in the hands of Thomas Johnes at the end of the 17th century, with important links to the family's Carmarthenshire estate at Dolaucothi, near Pumpsaint, where the mansion was equally important within the area. In fact it was still in existence until 1954, when it was demolished.

A further picture of settlement in Llanfair is provided by a 1669 marriage agreement[6] with regard to a large number of properties, together with their lands, in this and neighbouring parishes. Those included from Llanfair Clydogau were as follows:

Nant y Medd	Maes Clywedog
Melin Llanfair	Y Velin Vach
Tir Pen y Bont	Tir Pen y lan
Tir Lewis Goch	Blaen y Cwm
Tir y Courte	Tir y Coed
Tir Thomas ap Evan	Y Wern wen
Tir yr Hen Noyadd	Tir Llwyn y Keven
Blaen y Wern	Tir y Kae glas
Keven y Maylard	

Tir means land. From this list we can see a number of houses which are still in occupancy or use today. They include Melin Llanfair (the Llanfair Mill), Nant y Medd, Blaen y Cwm (Blaen Cwm), Y Wern wen (Waun wen), Blaen y wern and Pen y lan (Penlan).

Chapter Three 1600 to 1699

The wills of several local dignitaries[7] provide further evidence of the society that was Llanfair in the 17th century. Marmaduke Lloyd in his will of 1690 left £9.5s.4d, whilst Jenkin John Jenkin, in his 1700 will, left £29.1.10d in the form of animals and produce, plus property. Walter Prise of Glan y Wern, Llanvair Clydogy, in his will of 1693, is described as a "Gent". This important local house became Blaen y Wern and then Blaen wern and lies north of the Llanfair to Llangybi road.

Walter Lloyd of Olmarch[8] shows in his will of 1691, the important position of the parish church for the gentry. He also demonstrated his consideration for the parish poor upon his death. His will states:

"And my body to be.....Christian burial in the Parish Church of Llanvair Clydog
I give into the poor of the parish of Llanvaire Clydogy a fund of forty shillings, and by like fund to the body of the poor of the parish of Llanthewi Brevy".

The earliest written records of St Mary's Church are held in the National Library of Wales (NLW), and consist of a summary of baptisms, marriages and deaths for each of the years 1676, 1678, 1679 and 1684. The writings are very faint and extremely difficult to read. They are in English. Records for other years in this century have been lost.

Written evidence of the physical state of the parish, its church and the mansion is provided by E. Lhwyd in 1697[9]. Lhwyd's unpublished account was written in note form and contains many spelling inaccuracies. It was to form part of documentation for a planned, but never implemented gazetteer of Wales, which he hoped to write. I have extracted from his notes, the following key detail about the parish of Llanfair Clydogau:

- The parish's name is derived from the three small rivers (Clywedog) located half a mile east of the Church;

# Chapter Three	1600 to 1699

- The Church is dedicated to the blessed Virgin Mary; it is an impropriate church belonging to the Collegiate Church of Llanddewi Brefi; there is a curate;
- There are two wooded bridges across the rivers: one across the Teifi and the other the Clywedog;
- The House of Llanfair is located near the Church, occupied by Thomas Jones's, a young gentleman; whilst there is another gentry house in the parish at Blaen y wern;
- The ancient code of arms of the Llanfair gentry is fixed over the porch door of the House;
- Llanfair Mountain is famous for turf, which smiths use as if it is coal;
- Agriculture includes the growing of corn, oats and barley; there is woodland and poor grass; animals include cattle, horses and sheep;
- The parish population are healthy, since one resident, Catherine Lloyd is 90 years of age.

Over the years since Lhwyd wrote, a great deal of physical change has occurred to the parish, but the bridges, now built of stone, are still there. The general picture of the nature of the farming is still an accurate depiction until well on into the 20th century, as too, was the digging of peat. For instance, Tom Thomas[10], formerly of Gwarffordd and now Salisbury recalls how when as a boy in the 1930's, he accompanied his grandfather, Morgan Jones of Esgairddu to cut, dry and carry peat. They went onto the mountains, beyond the last cottage, Frondale, where a woman called Selina lived. This is the area on the slopes of Bryn Mawr, now in the possession of the Forestry Commission.

In summary, what we can positively and accurately say about society, agriculture and the economy during the period 1600-1699 based upon the existence of the quoted legal case documents and wills of the local gentry, and Lhwyd's notes is as follows:

Chapter Three   1600 to 1699

- the existence of a corn mill on the Llanfair Road, before 1669;
- the occupation of major houses in the parish by rich and powerful families, such as those of Walter Prise and Walter Lloyd;
- the existence of two major houses: Plas Llanfair and Blaen y Wern, occupied by local gentry;
- an economy developed around agriculture, but with trade occurring between farmers and the mill proprietor;
- the operation of a church located at a central point for communication within the parish and with an important spiritual and ritual role, especially in relation to burial;
- the existence of a group of extremely poor people for whom a donation of money upon the death of a leading member of society would have been vital.

In addition, the population was very small and scattered. Roads were very poorly developed and surfaced, and links with the rest of Wales and England were few. Life for the few gentry families, in comparison with the broad mass of the population, would have been relatively good. They would have had a regular income from the rents paid by their tenants, employed house servants, and had opportunities to travel outside the area. Another characteristic was that they would have spoken largely English, whereas their employees and their tenants would have been Welsh speakers. So important were some of these local families, that Llanfair provided during this century, one Member of Parliament and four High Sheriffs of the County. The detail was:

Member of Parliament:

- 1640, Walter Lloyd;

Chapter Three   1600 to 1699

the High Sheriffs were:

- 1603, John Lloyd;
- 1622, Walter Lloyd;
- 1656, Thomas Lloyd;
- 1674, Thomas Johnes.

The parish between 1700 and 1799

William III (died 1702); Anne (1702-14); George I (1714-27); George II (1727-60) ; George III (1760-1820).

Significant developments

1707 United Kingdom established; 1762 - Bridgewater Canal started; invention of steam engine; development of factories; 1785 publication of The Times newspaper.

A survey of parishes in Cardiganshire in 1707, shows Llanfair with the Rev. Daniel Rowland as curate of the impropriate church, (impropriate means where there has been a transfer of ecclesiastical revenue to a lay person). The parish population was described as consisting of only 23 families. Llangybi had 25 and Cellan 42 families[1].

A book published in 1721 by Erasmus Saunders[2] entitled, "A View of the State of Religion in the Diocese of St Davids: About the Beginning of the 18th Century, Together With Considerations of the Reasonableness of augmenting the REVENUES of Impropriate CHURCHES", shows the Llanfair Clydogau Church as "Llanvair Cludogie Church, Impropriate" It is listed as one of a large number of livings with a very small income. The exact amount is shown as £4 per annum. On the other hand, several neighbouring churches were richer. Kellan, or Cellan, is shown with a much larger income of £19, and Bettws Bledrws with £18. That would be a reflection of factors such as the size of its congregation, the number of rich benefactors and the value of the tithes that remained attached to the parish after the transfer of a large element to lay hands by the Crown after the takeover of the Church in the 16th century.

Overall, the financial situation was desperate for a great many of the churches within Cardiganshire. They did not have enough money to operate properly and maintain their buildings. Though Llanfair was shown as an

Chapter Four 1700 to 1799

impropriate church, there was no named patron shown. Saunders' comment on his survey of church finances, was that many of the parish churches in the St David's Diocese were financially impoverished and dilapidated. In a general statement of the plight he witnessed, he wrote:

"in some places we have churches without chancels, in others we have but some pieces of a church remaining...in some not only the bells are taken away, but the towers are demolished, and in many others there are scarce any seats....their little windows are without glass.....their roofs decaying, tottering and leaking, their walls green, mouldy and nauseous.....and their floors ridged up with noisome graves without any pavement, and only covered with a few rushes".

Further evidence of the dire state of a number of Cardiganshire churches is provided by a study by David Lloyd Davies: "Some aspects of the History of the Church in North Cardiganshire in the 18th Century". He comments on the situation in this general area. He said only three churches in the deanery could be given a first class certificate: Tregaron, Llangwyryfon and Llanbadarn Trefeglwys.

The desperate condition of some church finances led to the passing of Queen Anne's Bounty Act of 1704, which aimed at augmenting the maintenance of poor clergy. This Act provided for the use of the money currently being received by the Crown from what were called "first fruits and tenths", to be released and utilised to generate funds to improve the income of the poorer parishes, initially where the payment to the minister was less than £10. These first fruits and tenths were a tax which used to be levied by the Vatican upon churches, but which was taken over by Henry VIII and incorporated into Crown revenues. It was the implementation of Queen Anne's Bounty in 1714 which gradually led to an improvement of the Llanfair church finances. For instance, on four occasions during the 18th century, Llanfair parish church received £200 of Queen Anne's Bounty money for the purchase of property and land, with the intention of the rental being generated from this investment being used to raise the income of the minister. (the Bounty money was allocated to Llanfair in 1743, 1756, 1777 and 1794). As a consequence of this approach to investment, in 1809, the income of the Llanfair incumbent is shown as £83.14s.6d per annum, of which only £4 came from the lay owner (large landowner) of the tithes which were levied upon the population[4]. The bulk came from the investment made into properties and lands in the parishes of Llanwenog, Pencarreg, Llanbadarn Fawr and Llanwrda. These lands were known as Glebe lands.

We are fortunate in having access to the short written accounts of the few St Mary's Vestry meetings[5] (annual meeting of the parishioners), which have survived. Those remaining for the 18th century relate to 1782-4, 1793, 1794 and 1796. They give a little insight into the efforts being made by the few people in attendance, (for instance there were four people present in 1794), to seek to maintain the operational fabric of the church.

On the 7th April 1782 "It was agreed by the parishioners there to present the following articles to the Bishop's Court:

- Repairing the church wall;
- Item concerning the Chancel - a new door on the passage that leads from the Church to the Chancel".

On 21st April 1783 the items to report upon were:

- "The churchyard wall;
- Thatch the site".

On 12th April 1784 the meeting decided to "present to the Bishop's Court:

- The church to be repaired - a new pulpit and the churchyard wall".

At the 1st April 1793 Vestry meeting the decisions related to:

Chapter Four   1700 to 1799

- "The south side of the church wall to be pointed and mended;
- A few of the benches in the church to be repaired".

On Easter Monday in 1794 the Vestry gathering resolved:

- "That the church Chest be repaired; and
- The church door lock be properly mended".

On Easter Monday 1796 the Vestry meeting resolved the following:

- "A new shovel be made at the expense of the parish;
- The Chest lock be properly fixed ;
- The church yard gate be hanged up."

The only other information contained within the written account of the Vestry meetings is to detail the names of the churchwardens. These short Vestry notes were written in English.

At a general level, Diocesan information shows efforts were made, following the Saunders Report of 1721, to try to improve the finances of the more impoverished churches, with their low quality and badly maintained buildings. Nothing specific is shown about St Mary's in either the St David's records or the surviving Llanfair Clydogau records about finance, though as is outlined above, a greater income was being made available in terms of the salary of the curate as the century progressed. What is clear from touring writers, who wrote accounts of the area at the turn of the century, is that matters in relation to the church building and its site were still bad 80 years after the Saunders Report. Equally bad was the overall physical condition of the Llanfair parish in terms of appearance.

Though the population was small and most of the people extremely poor, information available shows the church was very much at the heart of the community, especially in the provision for baptisms, marriages and burials.

Chapter Four   1700 to 1799

Church records of baptisms, marriages and burials

Church records provide a valuable source of information about not only the position of the church within the everyday lives of the population, but also the economy, the social structure of society and prevalent attitudes towards personal behaviour. Records relating to baptisms, marriages and burials exist from January 1748. They are recorded using two different systems or approaches. Firstly, the detail appears in the 18th century in an adhoc and unstructured fashion, using an approach determined on the St Mary's church site by the two churchwardens who happened to be in post for that particular year. Secondly, from 1813, the records are set out in a clear and systematic manner in accordance with an Act of Parliament of 1812. This latter approach utilises a separate book for each of baptisms, marriages and burials.

Burial and interment within the church.

We know that people were, in the 16th-18th centuries, being buried within churches, and St Mary's was no exception. For instance, Walter Lloyd's will of 1693 referred to his request to be buried in the church in Llanfair, as did the 1586 will of David ap Jevan and that in 1592 of Jenkin Lloyd. Information is also available of other notable funerals at the church. The notes of the churchwardens, David Rees and Evan Williams indicate that on 9th December 1751, Thomas Johnes of Dolaucothi was interred. Another note of the churchwardens in 1784/5 refers to "Interred item. Captain John Johnes of Dolecothi, buried April 1785, as appears on the Monument erected in Llanfair Church by M.J. Hughes (Father's direction)"

These funeral entries within the Llanfair records indicate that interment did take place for members of the rich and major landowning families, of which the Johnes were particularly significant at this time. No complete and comprehensive list of these interments exists, nor is there any inscription evidence on the floor or walls of the church. If such written detail existed it was probably wiped out during the renovation of the building in the 1880's.

Evidence available from several sources suggests that there was indeed an operational vault within the church which is not visible or accessible today. In his 1903 account on Cardiganshire, George Evans[6] wrote: "In a large vault beneath the chancel are buried some members of the family of Johnes, of Dolaucothi". He points too, to the church records and to the use of the word interred rather than buried. This vault would appear to have been accessible up to the point of completion of the remodelling and renovation of the church in 1888. Iris Quan[7] of Blaen Cwm told me she recalled her father, who was a young man in 1888, telling her that he was invited to visit the vault before it was sealed, but had been unable to attend because of illness. Gwyneth Jones[8] of Noyadd told me that her grandmother, who was a little girl in 1888, had visited the steps leading down to the vault before it was sealed. See also account of A. C. Bradley[9] of 1903 below, which refers to the church's vaults and the Johnes family.

Llanfair Mansion (Plas Llanfair)

In terms of the owners of Plas Llanfair, we know that Thomas Johnes of Dolaucothi and Llanfair, married Jane Herbert of Hafod in about 1704. She inherited the Hafod Estate, located near Devil's Bridge in north Cardiganshire, and her marriage, inheritance and then early death soon after marriage, linked Llanfair with Hafod. Upon the death of her husband, who had no heir in 1733, the whole estate passed to the family of his cousin, Thomas Johnes of Penybont, near Tregaron. The deceased of 1733 in his will, described his main house as being Dolaucothi. He appointed his cousin Thomas Johnes to be the Executor and Trustee of the will[10] until his nephew, son of Thomas Johnes of Penybont, also Thomas Johnes reached the age of 21. He specified that the young named heir should receive £150 per annum until he reached the age of 18 and then, £200 per annum until he reached the age of 21. This large amount of money allowed him to live rather grandly until he was able to inherit the rich Llanfair Estate. It is

Chapter Four   1700 to 1799

understood that Thomas Johnes of Penybont took possession of the Llanfair Manor House in 1733-1734, along with his two sons, Thomas and John.

With his large personal allowance and subsequent income from the Llanfair Estate, Elizabeth Inglis Jones points to the young man's fulsome life as a visitor to London. She refers to his friendship with some of the major social figures of the age, a number of whom braved the long and difficult journey to Llanfair to join him and his social group in merriment at the Manor house and in its Estate. She states that they played cards, drank wine and in general lived a leisured, pleasurable and relaxed life. This would have been in marked contrast to that of most of the rural poor in the parish who were either tenant farmers on the Estate or farm labourers. She names the following leading figures of London society who stayed at the Manor House, sometimes for several weeks at a time: Sir Charles Hanbury Williams, Henry Fox (later Lord Holland), Richard Rigby and Thomas' cousins, the Lloyds from Peterwell near Lampeter.

A wedding agreement[11] relating to Thomas Johnes of Llanfair's planned marriage to Elizabeth Knight of Herefordshire in 1746, shows his father living at Dolaucothi and himself, at Llanfair. Building upon his own good and ample income, this agreement shows him planning to marry rather well. Soon after this agreement was signed, he married the said Elizabeth Knight of Castle Croft. She was an heiress who brought him a very large dowry of £70,000. She was the daughter of a rich iron master and upon the marriage, Thomas Johnes moved to Herefordshire to live at her parents' home with its large parkland estate, whilst also keeping his Cardiganshire estates. Croft Castle is now owned by the National Trust and a visit there shows elements on display of Mr and Mrs Thomas Johnes' life and a reference to Llanfair. The second brother, John, lived at Dolaucothi. In 1748, Thomas and his wife had a son, also called Thomas. He was the Thomas Johnes who became famous for developing the Hafod estate as a world renowned centre for upland farming techniques, afforestation, the distinguished architecture throughout his house and estate, his library, his famous visitors and his in-house printing press.

Chapter Four — 1700 to 1799

It seems likely that the decline in the Llanfair Mansion began soon after the switch in location of Thomas Johnes to Herefordshire in 1746. He did not visit Cardiganshire much after this date, but did seek to develop further, his business interests in the county. He was still an important Cardiganshire Freeholder in 1760, though with his main house shown as Ludlow in Shropshire. Elizabeth Inglis-Jones[12] believes evidence exists of his son, Thomas, having some personal physical presence in Llanfair Clydogau. The younger Thomas married his first cousin, Jane Johnes (the daughter of the afore mentioned John), of Dolaucothi, probably in 1783-4. The marriage detail cannot be found. Because of their close family relationship in being first cousins, there is a degree of mystery surrounding the circumstances and location of their marriage. The place of their child, Mariamne's birth on 30th June 1784, is also unclear. According to Elizabeth Inglis-Jones in her book, "Peacocks in Paradise", "tradition still lingers on in Llanfair Clydogau that the little girl was born in the old Manor house there, which her grandfather had deserted".

The close link between Llanfair, its church and the rich Johnes family is shown in the Vestry minutes concerning burial in the church quoted above. Further evidence of the accuracy of the interment referred to within the minutes, receives confirmation from Thomas Johnes' will of 1733. He states, "I do hereby desire that my body be interred in the parish church of Llanvayre Cledogge in the said County of Cardiganshire, in a private manner and that the whole expense of my funeral do not exceed £80".

Lead and silver mining.

The 18th century was the time when the main initial development of lead mining occurred in Llanfair. The type of ore which was found here contained not only lead, but also silver. It had the highest silver content of all the Welsh ores. The start date for the mining was in the 1750's. The baptismal records of the church provide some statistical record of aspects of the ebb and flow of this significant mining development. In fact, the records allow

Chapter Four   1700 to 1799

interpretations to be made, and conclusions drawn, with regard to most of the demographic, social and economic changes within the parish over the years since the most readable of the parish recording began in 1748. For instance, during the period 1748 -1758, the number of baptisms recorded in the church records was never more than four children in one year, but over the next ten years to 1768, the figure rose to six, seven, and nine, and in one year was 11, as the parish's economic base changed and the population grew.

This change was associated with the development of mining and the recruitment of men from other areas of Wales and elsewhere in Britain, such as Derbyshire, to undertake this work. The churchwardens in their recording of baptisms chose to add to their written note, the fact that the first miner's child to be baptised was on the 5th May 1759. It must have been a particularly important and unusual event in their minds since they did not make any mention of any parent's occupation until this date, and no other baptised child of that year had a similar record of parental occupation (it is presumed that those mainly came from an agricultural background). In 1760, four out of the six baptisms were miners' children. Presumably this reflected an influx of young families drawn by the prospect of work. The overall number of baptisms fell back from 1773 to a more normal one to five or six children per year, (with an average of two or three), until 1799 when it rose to nine, and for the first time there is a reference to a weaver's child. This mention of a weaver probably signified the development of the textile industry along the Llanfair Road in the vicinity of Pandy.

Various accounts of Cardiganshire mining state that the discovery of a lead (with silver) lode in the bed of the river Clywedog took place in 1760[13], and quote Chauncey Townsend as making the original discovery, working the site himself until 1777. However, the precise chronology of the development is unclear and we now know Chauncey Townsend did not become engaged until the initial development was well under way. Letters in the Dolaucothi papers[14] held at the National Library, provide much useful information about the early years. These letters written by Thomas Johnes of Llanfair and Croft Castle, show him owning the mine and indicate mining development earlier than 1760. In a letter from Herefordshire, to his brother John at Dolaucothi in January 1758, he wrote, "I am glad to hear I have so much ore at Llanvayre". Yet he complained strongly about the costs of his funding of the operation and alleged that the workers at the mine were stealing from him. In November 1761 he asked his brother to visit the Llanvayre site when his local agent Evan Lloyd "settles and pays the miners" in order that "you would endeavour to understand the accounts, so as to have some check upon them and that you may be satisfied I am not greatly cheated". In December 1761 he thanked his brother for "going to Llanvayre; among those thieves, 'tis impossible to prevent all manner of cheating. I am much at their mercy and they have no consciences".

Cheating and thieving was Thomas Johnes' overwhelming view of the behaviour of the workers in his lead and silver mine(s). One can imagine life amongst these miners living fairly primitively on the banks of the River Clywedog, with few facilities and working to dig underground in dark and wet tunnels following seams of ore. At the same time they needed to construct simple housing and ore processing buildings and generate enough wages to enable them to live and maintain a family. Conditions must have been extremely grim and unpleasant. Where to live, how to get food and how to maintain one's life in a new location would all have had to be faced and a solution found.

In March 1762 Thomas Johnes concluded he had experienced enough difficulties with the mine in trying to manage it directly (from Herefordshire) and decided to advertise for someone to undertake its management since "I am thoroughly tired of the work. It is attended with a great deal of trouble and the expense is very great". By March 1763 he was still writing to his brother complaining of the costs of running the mine, stating: "the balance is infinitely against me and it drains me consistently of a great deal of cash". But he has good news the same month in that he has "let my mine works at Llanvair" to Chauncey Townsend. He took responsibility in May 1763.

Chapter Four   1700 to 1799

Johnes described him as having "a very thorough spirit of mining". He seems to have energised the whole mining operation and brought to bear better management.

We know that the mining took place at several locations adjacent to the River Clywedog. It seems likely that there was no steady and simple consistency in its development, growth and operation, but that there were times of considerable growth interspersed by periods with less or no activity. Thomas Griffiths[15] of Blaen Cwm, wrote a short paper about mining in the Llanfair area. The paper is undated, and signed "son of the soil", rather than by his name and is believed to originate from about 1888/90. Its authenticity seems clear in that his daughter confirms it is his writing and the handwriting matches that of Thomas Griffiths who gave a sample of his signature upon becoming secretary of the Llanfair Agricultural Show in 1919.

He wrote of personally knowing two surviving miners and was able to describe the remains of mine shafts which he visited, but which today cannot be easily identified. His writings are the closest we have to a contemporary account of the mining developments. On the start of mining in Llanfair he wrote: "the saying is that a servant from the Llanfair Mansion one day found while washing, a stone with a large quantity of lead" and this led to exploration work for lead deposits. This statement fits in well with the story of development since it seems likely that elements of the Johnes family were still living at Plas Llanfair in the 1750's, and to start a mining boom, someone had to find a piece of ore in order to trigger exploration of the area.

With regard to the sequence of development after the discovery of lead and silver in the 1750's, various pieces of building construction took place, and this included shaft sinking to get at the ore. In addition, there was the building of crushing facilities for the extraction of lead and silver from the ore, as well as the work undertaken in the 19th century to develop a leat, called heolddwr in Welsh, which was aimed at providing a ready supply of water for the workings from sources higher up the mountain. The power for the workings came from water driven wheels. Also to be constructed were channels for the movement of water around the site of the process plant or "works" in the valley, near to Plas Llanfair. The channels are shown clearly on the 1844 Tithe map. There would have also been an increase in the number of houses constructed to place incoming workers. These would have largely been in the vicinity of the mining activities, around the area of what is today Silvermine Cottage, (formerly Office Fach). There would have been a demand for labour, specific mining skills, stone, wood, tools, accommodation, provisions and a reliable and dependable road system to move along, not only for the hive of exploration initiated by the discovery of the ore, but also its subsequent transportation out of the area for sale elsewhere.

We have no firm information about the overall size of the population of the parish in the late 1700's, except that, like many areas within Cardiganshire, there was a substantial influx of people associated with the lead mining industry, and that there was a switch away from a total dependence upon farming. In the early part of the century, there were 23 families in the parish, but by 1801, there were 308 people. This introduction of mining to the local economic base was significant, but did not challenge farming as the predominant employer. However, the overall structure of rural life was changed beyond all recognition. The population mix of the parish was also considerably altered as people came to work in the mines from other areas.

This influx would have also seen local Welsh speakers encounter some English speakers. Previously, their main contact with the English language would have been through the world of the Church where, though services were in Welsh, it seems evident that most written communication was through the medium of English. Individuals may also have encountered English through contact with the small number of gentry families living in the area, or more specifically through contact with the Thomas Johnes family at Plas Llanfair.

Chapter Four   1700 to 1799

The poor of the parish

The parish was the responsible body for the administration of the Poor Law in the 18th and 19th centuries. Across Cardiganshire there were 76 separate parishes. At this time there were no workhouses. Davies[16], in a History of Cardiganshire, states that occasional or casual relief was given to paupers in money or in kind, fuel, clothing, barley, potatoes, etc. The system of catering for the very poor must have been severely strained, especially during times of economic decline or failure of agricultural crops following a bad summer's weather. These people faced the most extreme form of hardship and poverty. Put simply, some of the poorest people in society sometimes had no home, no money and nowhere to go.

There is a dearth of information with regard to the numbers and nature of destitute and financially desperate people within the parish, to whom in common with the rest of the country, the general term "pauper" was applied. Evidence of the use of this term can be deduced from the church records. The St Mary's burial record for the second half of the century shows a number of people being buried within the graveyard to whom this demeaning term of "pauper" was ascribed:

- 17th July 1762, John Edward, pauper was buried;
- 2nd April 1763, Lydia Rees, pauper, was buried;
- 27th September 1764, John David, pauper, was buried;
- 15th April 1764, David, pauper, was buried;
- 20th February 1768, Mary Evan, pauper was buried;
- 14th February 1795, Timothy Thomas, pauper was buried.

Thereafter, there are no references to the term pauper in the church records. Funding for the very poor and destitute was a major problem as relief of the poor had to come from the residents of the parish. A parish which was, of itself, relatively poor.

Overall conditions for most of the population must have been very hard as they tried to make a living as miner, farmer or farm labourer. Wages were low, employment rights were none existent, support systems which we accept and expect today, were absent and the area in general, remained poor and isolated, with ill developed transport systems. In the 1750's, the wage of a male farm servant ranged from 90s a year for a head servant, to 40s for the third servant[17].

Llanfair crime

The parish may have been remote, relatively inaccessible and have had a small population of only 23 families at the beginning of the century, but it also suffered the complete range of crimes. The Records of the Great Sessions in Wales[18] provide interesting detail of alleged criminal activities brought before the courts. Some of the cases were as follows:

- William Williams, labourer of Llanfair, was accused of the very serious crime of theft of a horse. It was alleged he exchanged the horse with the Llanfair Clydogau inn keeper. The trial took place on 9th June 1733. He was found guilty and sentenced to death.
- Rees William, yeoman of Llanfair, was accused of assault in Llanfair. The trial took place on 18th March 1744.
- Jenkin William (yeoman) and his wife Winifred of Llanfair, were brought before the court on 6th May 1751 accused of: "riotously breaking and entering" the house of John William, yeoman.
- On 1st December 1786, the trial took place of Anne David of Llanfair. She was accused of the "murder of Lettice David, otherwise Thomas, widow, who was the prosecutor's sister, by beating her with a stick in her own home. The inquest detail records the death as murder by persons unknown". An accomplice was also indicted. Three others were also suspected of the murder, and

of burning the deceased, but were not indicted. Anne David was found not guilty.
- On 30th June 1791, David Morgan, yeoman of Llanfair, was tried for the theft of sheep. His prosecutor was local farmer John Walter of Llanfair.
- On 7th November 1791, there was another trial involving the theft of sheep when Llanfair farmer David John Morgan prosecuted David Jenkin of Llan y Crwys, Carmarthenshire.

Llanfair freeholders and leaseholders in 1760

Name	Place of abode	Place of freehold
Thomas Johnes, Esq(1)	Ludlow	Llanfair Clydogau
Evan David Jenkin (2)	Cwsswch	Cwsswch
Thomas Rees	Do.	Do.
Evan Rees	Pantynos	Pantynos
Evan John, carrier	Cwsswch	Cwsswch
Rees Thomas, miner	Yr Allt	Yr Allt
Richard Johnes, gent	Berllandeg	Annuity out of Cwsswch

(1) Thomas Johnes - father of Sir Thomas Johnes of Havod;

(2) Evan David Jenkin - a conversationalist and poet. He was a leading figure in the religious controversies of the period in Cardiganshire.

source: Historical Society of W. Wales Transactions, Vol 3 1913[19].

The Llanfair Clydogau Estate of Thomas Johnes of Havod in 1791

Farm	Acres.	Rods.	Perches.
Llanfair Desmesne	315	3	5
Blaen y Cwm	47	1	30
Penlan trawscoed	86	0	25
Waun wen uchaf	49	2	25
Waun wen isaf	73	0	30
Cwfswch	74	1	35
Park y noyadd	73	1	15
Tir y cwrt	24	1	5
Pentrelan	44	3	0
Tir y park	20	1	0
Tyn y coed	27	0	2
Llyast y bedw	1	1	20
Gwern y medd	163	2	15
Cefn moelallt	35	2	5
Pentre Llanfair	93	1	5
Fach Ddu	63	2	27
Pen y Caeglas	44	0	25
Kellan Farm	23	1	33
Glantivy	37	3	35
Tir y Gaes	3	1	20
Kellan Mill Caegarw Fe	16	2	10
Llanfair and Cellan parishes	1,323	1	7

source: Llanfair and Llanddewi Brefi Estates, by T. Lewis 1791[20].

Chapter Five — 1800 to 1899

The parish between 1800 and 1899

George III (to 1820); George IV (1821-30); William IV (1830-37); Victoria (1837-1901).

Significant developments

Growth of Methodism (established 1795) with its appeal of thriftiness and concern for social improvement; 1801 London population reaches one million; 1803-15 Napoleonic Wars; 1832 Reform Act extends voting franchise; 1833 abolition of slavery in British Empire; 1837 Rebecca riots in Wales; 1870 first Education Act; growth of factories and urban areas in Britain.

Fenton[1] in his book," Tours of Wales," of 1804-13 wrote:

"Leaving Llanddewi Church and its miserable village, rode as far as Llanfair Clydoge, a Mansion of high note about a century ago, but now in ruins, as well as the Church near, the Chancel Window of which seemed to have no glass in it. The whole landscape around, being fairly stripped of its woods, exhibited a most sterile and inhospitable appearance. Cross Llanfair Bridge, and after a fatiguing ride through a narrow bad road, reach Lampeter".

Merrick,[2] writing about 1803 in a book entitled: "The History and Antiquities of the County of Cardigan", also gave an account of Llanfair Clydogau. He wrote:

"It is mostly celebrated for the mine works it contains, which were formerly very productive, but are now too much under water to be of service. The church is a perpetual curacy, alternatively in the gift of the family at Crosswood, and R Price, Esq., M.P. for Knighton in Radnorshire, who

Chapter Five — 1800 to 1899

bought Lord Cunningham's tithes. The tithes of the parish are shared equally by these two families and they allow five pounds per annum to the curate. The church is dedicated to St Mary and the present incumbent is (1800), the Rev. David Williams. The building consists of a nave, chancel and porch. The font is a round basin with rude carving of men's heads, one at each angle. There was formerly a handsome monument to one of the Johnes, erected about the time of Queen Anne (1702-1714), but this has been destroyed by some workmen or miners employed near the church. There now remains one monument on a black stone to the north side of the nave, on which is inscribed the following:

"Underneath lie the remains of John, the son of John Hughes of Gwernmeth in this parish, who departed this life on the 27th of April 1785 aged 9 months. And also, Nancy, the Daughter of the aforesaid John Hughes, Gent. Who departed this Life Jan. The 16th 1799 in the 18th year of her age.

> Pain was our portion, Phisick was our food
> Groans were our devotion; drugs did us no good,
> Christ was our Physician, and knew what was best
> To ease our pain, and set our souls at rest"

So, as we begin to consider developments during the 1800's, we know from the above eye witnesses, that the church's tithe income had risen from the £4 of 1721 to £5 per annum in 1800 (and in addition, there was also some rental income from the Queen Anne's Bounty lands), but depressingly, damage has been caused to an important monument to one of the Thomas Johnes of Plas Llanfair; the mansion is in ruins; the church is in a state of neglect; the mines are operating only with difficulty because of water penetration; and the whole area of the parish has lost its trees and is bare and inhospitable. It sounds miserable and unattractive.

Other writers about rural Cardiganshire in the early 19th century give a depressing picture of the whole area. Barber[3] in his "A Tour of South Wales," comments on what he saw in Tregaron in 1803. He describes it as "a poor straggling ill built town…..it provides a pleasing relief to the surrounding dreariness" of the rural area. Malkin[4], also writing in 1803 about Cardiganshire, states of the people, " the ordinary appearance of things in their present state, is impoverished and hungry", and " their gains are small, their mode of living coarse in the extreme, their habitats squalid". He goes on to criticise the large number of absentee landlords who he feels contribute little to the economy and life within the county. He states: "It is a great misfortune to the northern part of the county, that although there are many ancient mansions, few of them are tenanted…….A person enumerated to me a list of proprietors, all immediately surrounding the neighbourhood, who drew out of the county, £25,000 annually, without ever seeing the spot from whence they derive their wealth; consequently without circulating any part of it either in hospitality, or in the judicious and liberal employment of the poor". 1817 was a difficult year for Cardiganshire since there was a famine and "the houses of some of the gentry were besieged by people wanting food"[5.] W. J. Lewis[6] wrote: "though the condition of those engaged in agriculture did improve after 1820, want was never far away from the door of the small farmer and labourer and there was little but sentiment and a fear of the unknown to keep the young people at home".

Llanfair crime

The records of the Court of the Great Sessions in Wales, held by the National Library and quoted in the previous chapter, give us a further insight into social conditions within Llanfair as the parish's population began to grow rapidly. A court case of 23rd March 1800 details Richard Davies (Labourer), Edward Jones (Labourer), Lettice Jones (Spinster) and Morgan Llewhellin (Labourer), who were accused of the theft of drink including rum and a cask.

Sale of the Llanfair Demesne

An auction sale took place at Garraway's Coffee House, Change Alley, Cornhill, London on Thursday 28th April 1803, of a large number of estates in Cardiganshire[7]. Lot 1 was described as "a capital, desirable and very profitable freehold estate, comprising Llanfair Demesne, sundry eligible farms, lands and tenements. Containing 1241 acres, with farm houses and outbuildings, lead works, mills and extensive sheep walks. In the occupation of tenants at will, at rents amounting to only £574.15s.0d per annum (capable of considerable increase)". The brochure for the auction then listed the Llanfair properties which were for sale, alongside the tenant, size and annual rent. The extract below has been compiled from the auction details. This auction of the Llanfair lands, and others in the parishes of Llanddewi Brefi, Caron, Kellan, Llangybi, Llandarn Odyn, Llangeitho, Bettws Bledrws, Kilkennin and Llanrhystud, constituted action being taken by Thomas Johnes of Hafod to release money from his then extensive estates. Thomas had succeeded his father, Thomas Johnes of Llanfair and Croft Castle, following his death in 1780. By the end of the 1790's, a number of his lands were mortgaged in order to fund his large and costly Hafod capital projects. Put simply, he needed cash to pay for his Hafod developments and his grandiose life style.

Extract from the brochure of the sale of Llanfair lands							
Farm	Tenant	A	R	P	£.	s.	d.
Llanfair Demesne	John Morgan	197	1	30	100	00	00
Llanfair lands	John Williams	11	1	25	11	11	00
Llanfair lands	Joseph Davies	15	3	30	11	00	00
Llanfair lands & mill	David Evans	9	0	20	31	10	00

Extract from the brochure of the sale of Llanfair lands (cont'd)							
Farm	Tenant	A	R	P	£.	s.	d.
Penlan Trawscoed + Llanfair lands	Thomas Richards	100	2	30	31	10	00
Blaen y cwm	David Davies	47	1	30	33	12	00
Llanfair lands	Jenkin Davies	67	1	15	13	00	00
Waun Wen Uchaf +Waun Wen Isaf	Edward Johns	122	3	15	65	00	00
Park y' Noyadd	Jenkin Davies	73	1	15	30	00	00
Cwffwch	Ann Able	74	1	35	21	00	00
Tiry Cwrt + Pentre r' Lan	John Evans	69	0	5	25	04	00
Tyny Park + Tyny Coed	Jonathan Marsden	47	1	2	22	00	00
Pentre Llanfair + Fach ddu	David John Morgan	160	3	32	100	00	00
Llyarty bedw	David Lloyd	1	1	20	2	02	00

Extract from the brochure of the sale of Llanfair lands(cont'd)							
Farm	Tenant	A	R	P	£.	s.	d.
Llyarty bedw	David Lloyd	1	1	20	2	02	00
Gwerny Medd + Pt of Peny Gae Gla's	John Hughes	166	2	5	40	00	00
Cefn Moylallt	David Williams	35	1	5	10	00	00
Peny Cae Gla's & Mill	Timothy Davies	41	0	35	27	05	00

(A = acres; R = rods; P = perches); (£ = pounds; s = shillings; d = pence *). (*pre decimalisation – 12 old pennies = 1 shilling; 20 shillings = 1 pound).

The "arrival" of Lord Carrington

The Llanfair estate, including the lead and silver mine, was sold to Lord Carrington, either directly at this time, or slightly later. It is clear that at about the same time, or soon after, Lord Carrington also bought other properties in Llanfair to add to his country estates in Cardiganshire. Yet he did not move to live in the area. In any case the premier property, Plas Llanfair, was not habitable any more being in a state of disrepair and collapse. His family held estates in the Home Counties and he managed his affairs in the Llanfair area through an Agent.

His purchase(s) gave him enormous power over the parish. He is shown on the 1839 tithe schedule as the largest single landowner with 35 separate Llanfair properties, a number of which were very large farms. Effectively, he

Chapter Five   1800 to 1899

controlled the tenancies and the rents paid. He also owned the Llanfair mines, though it seems likely that he followed the practice of Thomas Johnes in the 18th century in letting the commercial venture to a third party. The tithe schedule shows the mines with a tenant.

In addition to the rent he received, he was also entitled, along with his fellow aristocrat, the Earl of Lisburne, of Crosswood, to half the tithes paid by Llanfair residents. Apart from his economic power he also had considerable sway over the religious life of the community. Legally, he and the Earl of Lisburne alternatively appointed the vicar (curate) of St Mary's Church. He had the legal responsibility to make the necessary judgement about the personal qualities and attributes required of the incumbent and, without having to involve or consult anyone, he could make the next appointment to the parish. The parishioners had few rights with regard to this appointment.

Later we see his involvement within the parish, through the provision of land for the proposed and planned Capel Mair, and in matters concerning the controversy surrounding the St. Mary's vicar in 1859. The Llanfair estates were held by the 2nd Baron Carrington, until following his death, a new Baron Carrington, the 3rd in the aristocratic line, decided to sell his inherited properties in 1868.

The economy of Llanfair

With regard to the local economy, we know quite a lot from the national censuses which first began in 1801. In terms of employment and income, it was dominated by agriculture throughout the century. In 1801, 65% of the working population of Llanfair was in agriculture. In 1821, 81% of all families were "chiefly engaged in agriculture" before the proportion fell back to 67% in 1831. In 1841, the format of the census changed and the document began to provide greater detail of people's occupations. It recorded that 78% (119 persons) of the men worked as farmers, farm servants or agricultural labourers. The next largest group was lead miners at 11 persons. Very few

Chapter Five   1800 to 1899

women are shown as having an occupation in the first half of the century. Only 14 were listed as having an occupation in 1841 and 30 in 1851. They described themselves in the main, as a knitter of stockings or a house servant. The recorded censuses undervalue the occupational role of women.

Yet, censuses are invaluable in allowing us to see how much the parish's economy was self sufficient. Very few people moved far away from their home area to live. The parish was the most important social and economic aspect of their lives. The Teifi valley and its environs provided almost all the food a family would consume such as milk, eggs and meat, and also wool for the weaving or knitting of clothing, and skins for the making of shoes. Crops of oats, corn and potatoes were grown. Beer could be brewed and the parish had blacksmiths making horse shoes and metal implements for the farm and home. It also had tailors, dressmakers, shoemakers, corn millers and woollen processing sites. Fuel came from peat workings on the mountains. Most labour originated locally, except for elements of the lead mining industry, and people worked cooperatively and collaboratively in operating the few large, and many small farming enterprises, undertaking tasks such as shearing, hay making, sowing, potato picking and so on. As

A group of Llanfair women sewing in the late 19th century (one of those shown is believed to be Jane Pugh, dressmaker, of Pen Cilboa, sister of David and Anne Pugh)

the century progressed, the degree of self sufficiency began to change, with the arrival of the Manchester and Milford Railway to the edge of the parish, the foundation of a grocery shop and the opening of a school in 1877. But essentially, Llanfair was still a low income, very rural, isolated and largely self sufficient parish, even at the end of the century.

Health and the standard of living.

An 1864 Report[8] on the Death Rate in South Wales stated: "In Wales the difference between the living standards of the tenant farmer and the farm labourer was marginal only". In 1865 a similar report quoted a medical officer describing the children as "pining for want of food as soon as weaned" and thought that if the climate were cold, the whole race would perish. The report stated that there was an "utter impossibility of the peasants to earn sufficient to be properly fed". I. G. Jones[9] wrote: "The great houses of Trawscoed, Gogeddan and Nanteos contrasted sharply with the hovels of the mass of the peasantry". He added, "in Cardiganshire from the 1850's, the condition of life for a majority of the people was so appalling that religion was their penultimate refuge, the ultimate refuge was migration". The pattern in Llanfair probably reflected some of these comments, in that the numbers attending religious worship rose considerably in the middle years of the century. In addition, the practice of first working away, and then migration and the eventual abandonment of buildings and land holdings, gathered momentum in the latter half of the century.

The growth, then decline, of the population of Llanfair.

The majority of farms were small, and a large number were to be found in upland locations. The quality of the soils was mostly poor. The task of making sufficient of a living to support a family would have been daunting, and because income levels were largely very low, some of those working in agriculture often sought to supplement their income from working in mining,

Chapter Five — 1800 to 1899

in both the lead and coal mines. As the century went on and the lead extraction industry declined, mining activity was increasingly in the coal mines of South Wales.

The 19th century was a period of two distinct halves, in terms of the population, rapid growth was followed by a more gradual decline. The 60 year period 1801-1861, saw an increase in the parish population of almost 100% as the economy expanded. It would have been a time of considerable

Llanfair population statistics 1801-1901

Year	Population
1801	308
1811	360
1821	390
1831	385
1841	472
1851	595
1861	614
1871	593
1881	536
1891	512
1901	441

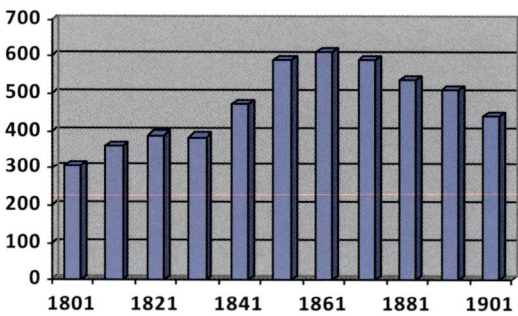

Chapter Five — 1800 to 1899

activity and change, as new people arrived and fewer people went away to seek work elsewhere, new houses were built and areas of the Crown lands, plus some "sheep walks" on the eastern uplands of the Clywedog valley, were enclosed and settled by industrious, poor, but optimistic farmers, hoping to make an economic living from some of the least profitable land in the area. However, with the decline of lead mining and a growing awareness of the difficulty with farming, the population fell back steadily from 1861, getting closer to its size of the early years of the century. This decline continued right through to the 1970's, and only began to be checked in the latter half of the 20th century, with an influx of incomers, mainly from England.

Accompanying the growth in population was an increase in the number of houses within the parish. In 1811 there were 79 and this increased to 131 by 1861, the peak year for the population. Thereafter, as the level declined as a consequence of people beginning to move away, the number of houses decreased to 112 by 1901. Some of this expansion and then decline is well recorded by the Rev. David Williams in a book entitled, Y Wladfa Fach Fynyddig[10] published in 1963. As a young man he lived at Esgair Crwys on the edge of Llanddewi Brefi parish, high above the Nant Clywedog Uchaf. He later became minister of Llanfair Dyffryn in Denbighshire.

He writes not only of this parish, but also of Llanddewi Brefi. His focus is upon the build up of population on the uplands to the east of the Teifi Valley in the middle years of the century. This population growth concentrated on the establishment of small holdings on some of the lands which had hitherto largely not been settled prior to about 1840. His main emphasis is upon the "tai unos" – houses built during one night on the Crown land which was unfenced. He points out that: "it was understood, as well as it being a custom, that if a house could be erected and completed in one night, and a fire made in it with smoke issuing from its chimney by the morning, that no one could interfere and eject the occupier, he being from that moment considered the sole and absolute owner". These hastily built huts were inevitably small, but once successfully established, were re built to a more satisfactory standard. This taking of the Crown lands, which were previously used as mountain pasture for lowland farms, occurred in many areas within Cardiganshire and often caused conflict between the "settlers" and the owners of larger and richer lowland farms. The Rev. Williams tells us that peace eventually came when the Crown Commissioners arranged for the selling and buying of these small holdings. Hence, in the eastern uplands of the parish we have today, a number of sites where farming was first established at this time. These sites were some of the most inhospitable and least attractive, with higher rainfall, thinner soils, lower temperatures and a more difficult physical terrain than the sites of well established farms on lower land. To settle these areas demanded an enormous physical effort from the pioneers in digging ditches to drain the land, removing stones and large boulders, constructing walls and field boundaries, felling trees, identifying and securing a well for a water supply and laying down roadways and field tracks. This work would have been initially, largely carried out by hand. The work would have been arduous, exhausting and back breaking, undertaken by an enterprising, determined and very poor group of people. They sought employment, an income and a greater degree of both independence and self sufficiency. The alternative facing individuals was to produce your own food (or work for an employer), versus having nothing to support yourself and family, and therefore, having to seek assistance from the parish and eventually, the Workhouse under the harsh Poor Law regulations. Workhouses were built later in the 19th century in Tregaron and Lampeter.

   The Rev. Williams identified 31 residences to write about within the eastern part of the two parishes, mostly at a height of about 900 to 1,000 feet, with Frondale at 1,100 and Castle Hill at 1,200 feet. I think that the actual number constructed from 1840/50 exceeds this, provided you take a larger area extending towards Cellan parish. However, he helpfully points out that all those which he writes about were occupied during his boyhood between 1880 and 1890. As a comparison, he writes that in 1954, only 10 of the 31 were occupied, and that by 1962, only five were still inhabited.

Chapter Five   1800 to 1899

Hence, we have the characteristic of a rapid growth in population through to 1861, with a spurt in house building and an increase in the farming of some of these more marginal and least attractive lands, followed by a slow decline during the remaining years of the 19th century. This was then followed by a very considerable decline in the population as people retreated from the eastern uplands throughout most of the 20th century.

The Llanfair residences which the writer specifies within his group of 31 are: Wenallt Ucha (Bryn), Pengelli'r Bryn, Blaenplwyf, Pengelli'r Esgair, Yr Esgair, Frondale, Castle Hill, Esgairddu, Esgairwen, Wenallt and Frondeg. In his book he recounts the various families who lived on these remote upland farms during his childhood.

As commented above, the movement of population out of Llanfair started as men began to work away from home in the coal mines of South Wales. This is evidenced by the census returns which show an increasing number of women left at home throughout Cardiganshire declaring their occupation to the enumerator as "coal miner's wife". These husbands went away in search of a higher income and came back at times during the year to join the family left behind tending the land. However, gradually the attractions of a more secure and greater income, plus urban living with less primitive facilities within the home, gained the upper hand and a drift of population away from the land took place.

At the end of the century, in the census of 1901, the proportion of a declining population involved in agriculture was still about the same as a hundred years before. The second largest occupational group for men was the woollen industry which employed five people. Amongst the women there were eight dressmakers. We can interpret the number of men working away, since on the day of the census, eight women described their occupation as "coal miner's wife" and in each case, no man is recorded as being present. No resident present described themselves as a miner, such was the decline in mining as an occupation in Llanfair.

Llanfair occupations

A general summary of the occupations in the parish is shown below in percentage format.

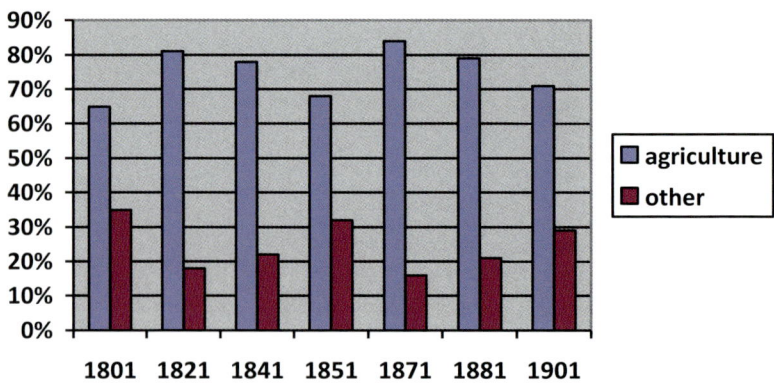

The figures for 1801 are the percentage of the working population, whilst the figures for other years, are the percentage of the male working population. As previously indicated, the census returns tended to underestimate working women. If women worked for a wage, then they are shown as having an occupation such as domestic servant or dairy maid, but the majority are not shown with an occupation, appearing as "farmer's wife" or "daughter", presumably receiving no formal wage, and yet in reality, would have been employed on the family farm or smallholding in an unpaid capacity. If the women who describe themselves as a farmer's wife or daughter are included in the occupation statistics, then this adds further confirmation to the tremendously important position occupied by agricultural occupations and activities within the parish.

Lead (and silver) mining.

Though Merrick had written of the mines as being in a state of decline in the early 1800's, it is clear as the century progressed, that the mines and their works recovered from this, with new investors, owners, leaseholders, managers and techniques deployed to deal with water penetration. These developments involved using water power taken from the Clywedog to propel various large drive wheels in order to assist the extraction of underground water and aid access for workers, plus the raising of the ore. The largest number of lead miners shown within the Llanfair census was in 1851, when there were 18 men or 13% of the employed population. However, it seems likely that it had been greater at some point before 1841. Earlier census returns do not help us determine numbers since 1851 was the first year which listed a precise occupation against a person's name. There is a suggestion below that the mines did employ more people at an earlier date. After 1851, the industry began to decline and a few years later, the population also began to go down, not only in Llanfair, but across the whole of Cardiganshire, as lead mining declined and in many locations, ceased. By 1871 there were only two lead miners shown on the census for the parish and two coal miners, the latter making a living in South Wales when not at home in Llanfair.

Since children were not recorded as having an occupation on the census form of this date, but many of them would have worked alongside their parents, it is fair to assume that the real figures for the separate employment groups were higher than the statistics referred to below would suggest. Hence, the statistical high point within the 19th century for lead mine employment of 18 persons in 1851, could in fact almost certainly be increased by several more, with the inclusion of family members such as women and boys. We have no record of numbers within the previous century, and the censuses from 1801 until 1831 do not specify occupation types, other than as a division into three groupings, "persons chiefly employed in agriculture; persons chiefly employed in trade, manufacture and handicraft; all other persons not compared in the two preceding classes".

Miners' children continued to be baptised in St Mary's church in a steady number throughout most of the first three quarters of the century. During most years there is a mention of miners with reference to baptisms of their children. However, in 1845 there was a surge in that 11 out of an unusually high figure of 22 baptisms in total, were miners' children. In 1849 the figure was even higher at 12 out of 17. These figures were very much against the norm for the period in terms of total annual baptisms which were mostly six or seven, largely farmers' or farm workers' children. It is suggested that they are indicative of a surge in activity in the mines in Llanfair in the late 1840's. Thereafter, the figures for baptisms of miners' children declined in the late 1850's and 1860's to a norm of one, two, or three to four children. The last child of a miner to be baptised was in 1874. Some statistical information on the mining of lead and silver at the Llanfair Mines during the 1840's is shown below [11]:

Production date	Ore (tons)	Lead (tons)	Silver	Value
1845	158	103	0	0
1846	242	157	0	0
1847	291	189	0	0
1848	80	53	0	0
1849	206	134	0	0
1850	88	67	0	0
1851-4 no detailed return				

In terms of further detail on lead miners and mining, we are indebted to Thomas Griffiths of Llanfair, quoted above. The background to the mining industry was that the landowner either employed someone to work the mine, or leased out the land on which the mine stood, along with the land around

Chapter Five 1800 to 1899

it, to a tenant. Sometimes the tenant worked the site, but on other occasions he hired a manager to organise and undertake the work. The direct employment approach was adopted by Thomas Johnes, from his Herefordshire estate in the 1750's and early 1760's. Thomas Griffiths offers us detail of some of the main operators of the mine. He wrote that the 1820's were the time of the mining engineer/manager, Jonathan Marsden, who lived at Gelli Ddyfod, "the first (person) that we know for certain, worked the mine at Silver Mine. They (the family), only worked the Gelli side of the river and only from the 10 fathom upwards mark, as far as the river would allow". Another researcher believes that Jonathan Marsden took over the mine in 1807[12]. It is unclear whether he was the tenant (of Lord Carrington, the landowner), or merely manager of the operation for someone else. Whatever, he did well financially from his mining activities. Confirmation of this is provided by a writer of 1870[13] who draws attention to the large profit that Mr. Marsden made.

From information within the St Mary's Church records of baptisms, marriages and burials, as well as from his will, we know that Jonathan Marsden worked the Llanfair mine until his death in 1837. Thomas Griffiths wrote that the working then transferred to Dr. Guinn (ended 1843), then Captain Francis, working for the then tenant of the site, John Taylor and Son. He was followed by Captain Poll, also working for Taylors, and then by Captain Ball, with the Taylors as tenants. Hall, in his writings tells us that the Taylors worked the mine until 1850 and then re opened it in 1860-62. The records do not allow us to report clearly the full sequencing by date, of the various leaseholders or tenants of the site, or who was working the mines between 1850 and 1860. Documentary evidence quoted below, also shows the Reverend Morgan Williams of Llanfair, having an involvement with the mine in 1839 as tenant, but for how long and the nature of his relationship with the workings is unclear. The writer of 1870 quoted above says that the site was not worked after about 1861. He reports that the deepest point reached was 90 fathoms and that over its lifetime it yielded £75,000 of lead and 900,000 ounces of silver. He asserts, "The mines are left with a rich lode on the 90 fathom level and any individual or company, disposed to lay out a moderate capital, cannot fail to return a large profit". This comment is in keeping with the entrepreneurial optimism of the time in the mining world.

Thomas Griffiths states, "when Marsden started, he got an old miner from Hendirmwyn to work here, and under him were placed local men. This miner was the great grandfather of David Jones of Brynmeinog. He made his home at Tyhen (by Pentre), which was almost in ruins then, no one would give him lodgings." He wrote that one of the later mine managers, Captain Francis, lived at "Cellan cwrt, then a nice house, and the whole of the field now in front of the house was a beautiful garden and orchard".

Remains of a mining tunnel in the Clywedog Valley (August 2008)

He stated that, "Under Captain Poll it was in full swing and employed about 200 hands, men, women and boys." If this fairly large figure is correct, it did not last long. As commented upon above, no census details document such a large occupational group living within the parish. The surge in employment could have been short lived and not coincided with any of the ten year census dates.

We do not have any surviving mine company records. Some researchers of mining in Cardiganshire suggest that 1862 was the last date upon which mining took place, and that upon the liquidation of the mine, it was bought for £750 by John Taylor's company and the mining equipment transferred to workings at the Lisburne mines to the north. However, Thomas Griffiths suggested some work took place later in the century. He wrote that: "the last time it was worked was under Mellor in 1872-4 with only about a dozen men, they only cut the level by Ty Powder, but got no lead". He provides us with detail of the use of various houses associated with the mining. " Office Fawr was used as an office, Office Fach, a smithy, with another three houses opposite the bridge and a tavern".

"From Captain Poll's time, Office Fawr was used by him and his family, Office Fach, then a smithy, he rebuilt for his office, the upstairs rooms only, and the room on the left downstairs was used to keep the safety equipment and candles, and the other room for drying the Captain's clothes. A large

Office Fawr in 2008. (now called Clywedog Cottage)

new smithy was built sufficient for three smiths to work in. Rhiw was built for the manager of the washings or floorings as it was called. There was a house for the grinding mill, a long house where the lead was stored before its carting to Aberaeron, and also a shed for the landing wheel, with a few smaller ones for the workmen to use for shelter. Capital building stones were had from the quarry in Gelli field."

He wrote that all the machinery was worked by waterpower from the Clywedog in Wauncafan, a small inlet by Cwm, and travelled by a ditch downhill. "It first of all turned the pumping wheel at the far end of the works in Cwm Gelli near Cwm, and right along from there, ran the rods placed on high posts, similar to telegraph posts, to the pumping shaft in front of Office Fach". In summer time, when the Clywedog had a low flow, then water from the mountain lake could be taken. This is the lake called Llyn y Gwaith at a height of about 440 meters (1,450 feet) on the Ordnance Survey map of today. He writes that it was built especially for this purpose by Captain Poll.

He also referred to the development of a leat or heolddwr to carry this water. Lewis[13] in 1833 indicated that mining was taking place at a depth of 250 feet underground and drew attention to the problems the mine faced during very dry weather because of a low volume of water in the Clywedog. This would help explain the construction of Llyn y Gwaith later in the century.

Llyn y Gwaith, created for the Llanfair mine(s)

Chapter Five   1800 to 1899

Thomas Griffiths referred to the "heolddwr on Bryn Cysegrfan (or Bryn Penlan), which is now used as a road, but which once brought a good share of the waters of the Clywedog, and had its mouth a little below Graig Ddu Uchaf and ran alongside the side of the mountain". He added: "some say that the heolddwr was to bring water to the Pysgodlyn which belonged to the Johnes of Llanfair Fawr and is still to be seen today in one of Blaen Cwm's fields, within the great park wall that they built for the deer, hence the name Cwm yr ewig". Archaeological survey work has been undertaken to try to find out more about this feature.

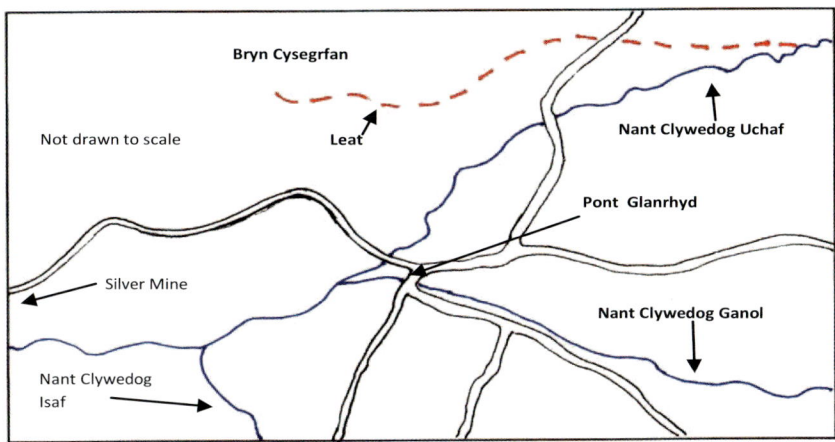

The Nant Clywedog and its channels for mechanical power

Photograph taken in 2008 showing position of the leat on Bryn Cysegrfan

Simon Timberlake, [14] who undertook this survey work, asserts that it ran from the Nant Clywedog Uchaf for about 1.5 miles, following the 280 meter contour line, before ending on Penlan land. Physical sections constructed across the route of the leat have allowed the researcher to state that the feature was a rock cut channel about 0.45 m deep, with an uneven boulder and clay filled rock cut floor. He could not ascertain a route beyond this point, hence he speculates that, "the leat was probably cut for the purposes of supplying water for mining, either for hushing, or to power a waterwheel for pumping or drawing water from a shaft. In the event, these two activities were either never carried out, or else the project(s) were abandoned very soon after they were started". He cannot find evidence of any intended mining occurring on this upland area. Austin[15] has also tried to find an answer to the conundrum of the route of this leat. Like Timberlake, he could not find any western extension beyond that on Penlan land, nor could he ascertain an eastern end. He also points out that, assuming the leat did run to the western edge of the upland overlooking the River Teifi, it would end its gentle downwards pathway on a very steep slope overlooking the lead and silver mine workings below. Questions to ask include: how would the water be transported downwards? Where would it be stored? Why would water be taken downwards by this route when it could reach the same spot of the mines storage ponds via a natural flow down the main River Clywedog if released from the leat earlier?

Hence, the available research evidence shows clearly that the leat did exist, but that it ended its route on the hillside. Austin points out that the 1853 Enclosure Award map shows the feature as a carriageway for traffic, although this was probably a secondary use.

The map below shows the silver mine workings and also details additional channels for the carriage of water adjacent to the workings. The map, which shows the pond or reservoir upstream from the mine workings, along with channels near to the river is based upon the detail provided by the 1844 Tithe Map of Llanfair. The remains of some of these channels can still be seen close to the Clywedog on land to the rear of Llanfair Fawr. This

Chapter Five 1800 to 1899

discharge route channel is stone lined, but today empty, and in places filled with earth. In the same general area there is evidence of mine waste or spoil. The amount remaining has been reduced a great deal by human extraction. Arwyn Evans[16] of Llanfair Fawr told me his father Gwyn had said that Ministry of War workers had taken a lot of the mineral waste from the site during the Second World War as hardcore for a road improvement scheme at Creuddyn Bridge on the Lampeter to Aberaeron Road. It was necessary to strengthen the road and secure improvements since it handled military vehicles travelling to a firing range near Aberaeron.

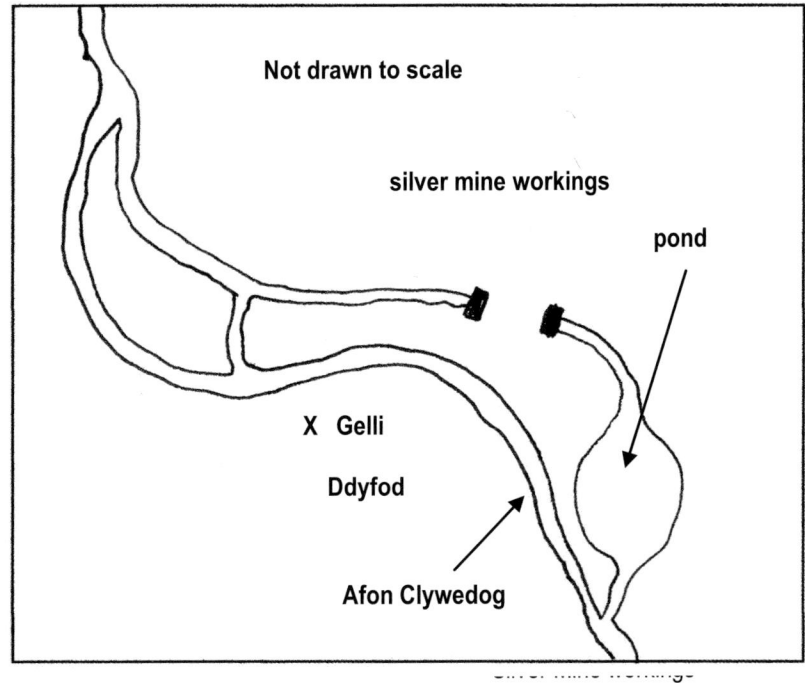

Distribution of water to the silver mine workings

Chapter Five   1800 to 1899

Jonathan Marsden of Llanfair Mines

Jonathan Marsden died in May 1837 and is buried in Llanfair Churchyard. His grave headstone states that he was a "Gent" of "Llanfair Mines" and was 84 years of age at the time of his death. He came to the area from

Inscription on the above gravestone "To the memory of Hannah, wife of Jonathan Marsden of Llanfair Mines, gent, who died on 11th August 1834, aged 52 years. Also the above named Jonathan Marsden who died on 23rd May 1837, aged 84 years.

Derbyshire to work in the Cardiganshire lead mines. In 1803 he was a tenant of two properties, Tyny Park and Tyny Coed in Llanfair, together with their 47 acres of land. In terms of the history of Llanfair he was a very important figure. He was a major employer who had considerable skill in mining techniques. He was also entrepreneurial and over a period of some 30 years, took actions which helped to shape not only the lives of many people, but also the pattern of development and settlement within the parish which grew up during his time, and which also endures today. Significantly, he did

Chapter Five — 1800 to 1899

very well financially from working the mines. Lewis[17], writing in 1833, recorded that the mine was worked very successfully from at least 1813-33, with goodly amounts of pure silver raised within the ore.

Jonathan Marsden's will[18] provides valuable information about his personal wealth and relative position within a society in which most people would have been extremely poor. The first thing to note is that he was, like many others, unable to write his name and, as a result, signed his last will and testimony with a cross. Secondly, at the time of his will being made in 1837, he lived some distance away from the mine at Powell Hill, just off the Llanfair Road towards Lampeter, on the extremity of the parish. Yet, clearly his main claim to local, and indeed regional importance, was his working of the mines, since that is what is emphasised on his grave stone. Thirdly, his bequests show the relatively large amount of money he had amassed in his lifetime. The detail of the amounts he left to members of his family, excluding the Powell Hill property, is as follows:

- Youngest daughter Anne £100 plus the furniture in the house;
- Daughter Mary Anne £200 plus a feather bed;
- Son Richard £50;
- Son Harry all the live and dead stock and implements of husbandry of the farm;
- Son Andrew £50;
- Son William £50;
- Son David £200;
- Son Benjamin £50 plus a silver goblet;
- Son Thomas £50;
- Daughter Sophie £10;
- Son John one shilling;
- Son Jonathan £50 plus a silver goblet;
- Son Anthony £200;
- Hannah, the natural daughter of his late son George, £10.

Chapter Five — 1800 to 1899

The actual distribution of money to his 13 surviving children might seem to be little unusual, ranging from bequests of £200, to one shilling. In addition, on top of the cash they were to receive, they were all to get an equal share of the sale of Powell Hill. In terms of the distribution of cash from Mr. Marsden's estate, the amount referred to was £960.1s.0d. Expressed in terms of the value of money today, this was equivalent to about £75,000 to £80,000. Excluding his farm, its implements and stock and his furniture, this was a great deal of money. It is indicative of the income and profits he was able to generate from the Llanfair Mines as a very successful operator.

We can trace a little more of the life of Jonathan Marsden from a search of the church records of baptisms. In 1815, his daughter Mary Anne was baptised, with Jonathan Marsden's home then shown as Gelli Ddyfod. He was described as "miner and farmer". However, this description of himself changed over time, so that by 1820 when his daughter Anne was baptised, his abode is shown as "Llanfair Mines" and his occupation is recorded as "Gent". His son George also had a daughter Anne baptised in the church in 1821. He too, showed his home as Llanfair Mines and his occupation as "Gent".

The significant position of the mines within Llanfair society can be seen by a reference to the church burial records for the churchyard. These show that another son of Jonathan Marsden, Stephen, also of Llanfair Mines, was buried on 28th November 1824, aged 30. Unusually his entry in the church record book was presented as evidence to the Court in Cardigan as part of a legal case on 5th May 1825. It is assumed there was an accident.

Accidents were a problem. The burial records of the church also include an entry of Rick Davies of Pandy who was buried on 27th April 1829, aged eight and "who fell into the shaft near Llanfair House". (believed to be a reference to Plas Llanfair). There is also a reference to another serious accident at the mine in as much as it is recorded that David Lloyd of Mountain Gate, was buried on 17th November 1842, aged 22, "who was killed by the wheel of the mine".

Chapter Five   1800 to 1899

Manufacturing and grain processing on the Llanfair Road.

In 1871, the other occupations besides agriculture within the community included masons, carpenters, a shoemaker, tailors, dressmakers, a miller, a hatmaker and woollen textile workers.

Physical evidence available today, shows a leat running from the River Teifi across fields and parallel to the Llanfair Road, leading to what was then, in sequence, Pandy Fulling Mill, Llanfair Mill and lastly towards a factory building or buildings associated with the woollen industry.

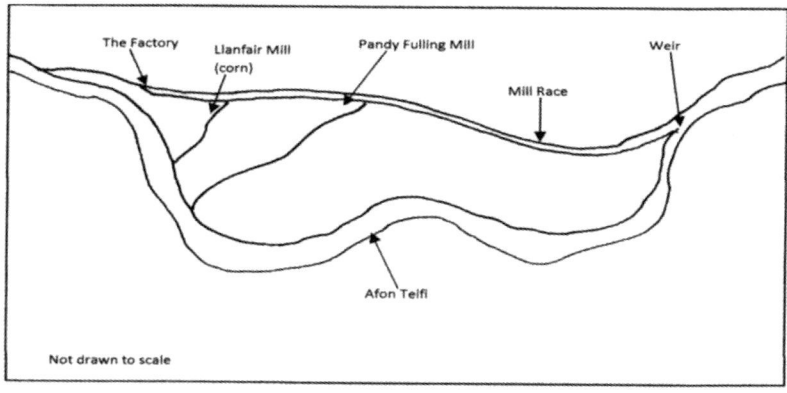

Route of Llanfair Mill leat

The leat or elements of it, must be very old, since we know from the earlier quoted Bronwydd manuscript papers, that a Llanfair Mill existed in 1669 and would have had to have power to operate its grinding wheels. The mill is also referred to in a Crosswood (home of the Earl of Lisburne), manuscript of 1772. In 1816 John Morgan was born there and his parents were tenants of the mill. In 1865, in order to be able to undertake more business for local farmers, he installed two additional grinding stones. The mill has not been in use commercially since the 1950's. It is a first class example of a rural Cardiganshire mill, and both the building and its operational machinery, including its water wheel, are still intact today.

Llanfair Mill leat

Water wheel at Llanfair Mill

Llanfair Mill

Chapter Five   1800 to 1899

Pandy is referred to as Llanfair Tucking Mill in a Crosswood Manuscript of 1772, and as Pandy Fulling Mill on the 1891 Ordnance Survey map. By the time of the 1982 Ordnance Survey map it was simply called Pandy. The development of Pandy in the 18th century had seen its use in connection with the woollen textile industry continue throughout the 19th century and into the early years of the 20th. Fulling or tucking is a stage in woollen cloth making which involves the cleaning of cloth to get rid of oil, dirt and impurities and at the same time, to thicken it. Here the cloth would have been beaten by wooden hammers which were powered by a waterwheel, and also scoured by water in order to clean the cloth. A fulling mill in Wales was called a pandy.

Pandy, formerly a fulling mill

The 1841 census shows the house, Pandy, as the home and working base of a man who describes himself as a clothier and weaver, whereas the 1891 census, shows a clothier in residence along with two other workers. The woollen processing ended at Pandy in approximately 1925.

The third of the commercial buildings located near to the Llanfair Mill is shown under various names. The house Llwyn Piod is shown as being occupied by a wool carder in 1841, whilst in 1871, two buildings located nearby, are called "The Factory" and are recorded as the home and working

Chapter Five
1800 to 1899

base of wool carders and a wool merchant, (between them employing some five people). By 1901, Llwyn Piod has a wool carder in residence, a building called the "Factory" a woollen spinner, and a separate building called Weavers Hall, a woollen weaver. The woollen manufacturing associated with these various buildings, which some of the records describe by the general title of Factory, (OS map 1891), ended in approximately 1927.

The Rev. David Williams, in his 1963 book referred to above, writing of life in Llanfair in 1880-90, mentions that John Abel was in charge of the Llanfair woollen factory, whilst Owen Jones was the weaver who lived close to the factory, and John Jones was at "the Pandy" (John y Pandy). He says the Llanfair area contained several noted tailors at this time, and names Walter Jenkins of Office Fach, (former lead mine company building) at Llanfair Clydogau. The Jenkins tailoring family were still operating upstairs at Office Fach in the 1920's, producing suits and dresses for local residents[19].

Though the woollen industry development was important, overall it paled into insignificance alongside agriculture. By 1881, 89% of the then declining working population were working in agriculture. No one was working in lead mining and three men were engaged in the woollen textile industry in the vicinity of Pandy on the Llanfair Road.

An indication of the nature of the local agriculture and working conditions is provided by the newspaper story in the Welshman[20], of a major fire which occurred at Nant y Medd on 24th June 1859. Fire was noticed at the farm at 3.00 am and had started in the barn, caused by:

" the incautious use of a candle by Jenkin Davies, nephew of Mrs Hannah Morgan the farm occupant, who at about 2.00 am, returned home with a load of lime, and being in the habit of sleeping in the barn, went there with a candle and asleep, leaving the candle burning.......the barn was totally destroyed. The fire also burnt wheat, barley, oats and hay in stacks in the farm yard". The damage was quoted as being £200.

Chapter Five   1800 to 1899

Shops and retail activities

A study of the census returns from 1841-1901 is revealing. In 1841 the parish had no shop, but did have two blacksmiths. As the economy grew and became more sophisticated by 1851, there were five blacksmiths, an inn at the Silver Mines, and at Llanfair Bridge, a draper/grocer. In 1871, the inn had gone, along with the mines. There was also a butter merchant at Llwyn Piod at this date. The inn was replaced by the Llanfair Bridge Inn which appears in the census, described as such for the first time in 1881, and was the home of Thomas Davies. John Evans had become the shopkeeper by this time at the Bridge, and there was also a grocer's shop at Glanrhyd, on the edge of Llanfair Mountain. In addition, there was an egg dealer at Oxen Hall, a tailor at Office Fach, a boot/shoemaker at Pentre Cottage and blacksmiths at the Silver Mine and Llwyngog. In 1891, the inn and grocery businesses were still at Llanfair Bridge and in addition, there was a grocer at Cwrt y Cylchau and two blacksmiths and a tailor in the parish. In the 1901 census, the inn was no longer shown as operating, neither were the shops at Glanrhyd and Cwrt y Cylchau, but the Llanfair Bridge shop was operated by Mary Evans and there was a tea merchant at Penygraig. There was also a shoemaker at Pantyresgair and blacksmiths at the Silver Mine and Llwyngog. No later further census details outlining houses and people has yet been published. The next will be for 1911 in 2011.

Education in the Llanfair area

Education provision was ill developed and largely nonexistent for the mass of the population throughout most of the 19th century across most of Cardiganshire. An official report[21] covering 1819-1837, on charities, provides some valuable information on provision. Llanddewi Brefi parish had the 1790 David Thomas charity, whereby he funded a meeting house for a school and bequeathed 40 shillings annually for every teacher employed.

The report stated: "the meeting house is a small building and the school is

Chapter Five   1800 to 1899

Llanfair Bridge Stores, a comparison : 19th century and June 2008

Chapter Five　　　　　　　　　　　　　　　　　　　1800 to 1899

now taught in it. On Sundays it is used as a place of worship by members of the Established Church, the dissenters having built a chapel for their own use. The present school master is Thomas Jones...he teaches 16 poor children of parents resident in the neighbourhood, some of whom are dissenters, and others, poor persons belonging to the Established Church. The children are taught reading, writing and arithmetic gratuitously, except that the parents find books and stationery. The master is allowed to take pay scholars and now has about 10". In 1782 Catherine Radcliffe gave another financial bequest to the school to assist with the funding of poor children.

Llanfair had nothing comparable to the Llanddewi development. Instead, several small private schools were founded which were located in the individual homes of the more educated people. This small development focused mainly on provision for boys. There is no totally accurate record of this initiative, nor any information as to how long the "schools" existed. However, a piece written by Dan and Aerwen Griffiths of Pengarn in Clonc[22] mentions a school for girls being opened in Office Fach in 1840 by an English woman called Miss Pierce. They refer to another at Y Plas, near Gwarffordd, operated by Evan Davies in 1848 and another at Troedybryn in 1845/55. William James started a school at Ysgoldy'r Mynydd in 1863. This is the same man who opened the Board School in 1877.

We are afforded a further insight into the lives of people in the Cardiganshire area through the work of the Education Commissioners of 1847[23]. The Commissioners' task was to visit and inspect every school in operation in Wales and at the same time, report on the character and conditions of the population and, "to form some estimate of the general state of the intelligence and information of the poorer classes in Wales". Another part of their remit was to look into "the means afforded to the labouring classes of acquiring knowledge of the English Language". The Report when published in three blue volumes, was known as the "Blue Books" and its content produced a very hostile reaction across Wales because of its criticism of the Welsh language and its comments upon the economic and social conditions of the people, and in some cases, their way of life and morals. However, Saunders Lewis[24] has referred to the document as "the most important 19th century historical documents we possess".

Some references from the Blue Books which relate either to Llanfair or the nearby local area are quoted below. In 1847 the parish did not have a school, unlike Cellan and Llanddewi Brefi where a few children continued to receive an education provided their parents paid. Others were taught free of charge under the terms of the Thomas Charity outlined above, following selection by the vicar. Conditions in most of the very limited number of schools in the area were bad.

Commenting on the Llanddewi Brefi school room the Commissioners said "furniture consisted of one small table for the master, two larger tables for a few of the children and about five benches, all of which were in a wretched condition". In Cellan, the Commissioners' assistant found: "the room in which the school was held was a small room, 12 feet square. The furniture consisted of 2 chests of drawers, 2 tables, 2 benches and 2 chairs. The floor was made of lime and sand". The questions which the staff of the Commission asked the children, were often English centred, and focused upon the teaching of religion. Often the questions were in English, whilst the children predominantly spoke Welsh. Hence there were frequently both translation problems and straightforward misunderstandings. The main comments about Cellan, where the school was closed on the day of the visit, involve the Commission's assistant writing as follows:

"On my way through the parish I met some children, whom I questioned. They had heard of God. He was in heaven. He had a son. His name was Jesus Christ. Did not know what sort of place heaven was. Did not know for what purpose Christ came to earth. Had heard of the Apostles. Did not know who they were. Cardiganshire was the name of the county in which they lived. Did not know the name of the adjoining county".

In terms of 21st century society today, this focus upon the Bible seems strange. Yet, the whole tenor of the inquiry had a strong religious theme. All three of the Commissioners were Anglicans, as were many of their assistants and most of the schools they visited were church foundations, either Anglican or nonconformist (who were referred to as dissenters). In addition, the Commissioners were English and spoke no Welsh. When it came to collecting evidence, a great amount came from vicars or other Establishment figures such as magistrates or the gentry. The general view is that the report has a strong slant against anything that was not Anglican Church or Establishment orientated. Yet Anglicanism was not the predominant religious preferment of the people, since, throughout the 19th century, there had been a steady and substantial growth in the numbers attending non conformist or dissenter churches. This trend was in strong evidence in Llanfair with the operation of the Anglican St Mary's Church and Independent Capel Mair. Essentially, across Wales this was a major religious divide between the Establishment church with its power and status, and the dissenter or nonconformists with their greater numbers. The 1851 Religious Census suggests that three quarters of the people in Wales attended nonconformist places of worship[25].

In another comment on Llanddewi Brefi, the Commissioners' visiting assistant checked on the standard of education of some boys and wrote:

" I heard them read the 48th Chapter of the Prophesies of Jeremiah, which they did miserably; false pronunciations were made in almost every verse...Afterwards I heard the same boys read a part of the 3rd Chapter of the Gospel of Matthew, which they did wretchedly, making false pronunciations, raiment being pronounced rimaint; wrath as hwrath".

It is not difficult to see why mispronunciation might have occurred. This astonishing focus upon the Bible, not only as a source of knowledge, but also as a supply of reading material, remains surprising to an educationalist today. Yet schools had few books, and the Bible would often be used as the main classroom reading material for the few who attended these places of learning. What we don't know is how many books were available, or whether the reading required was in Welsh or English.

Chapter Five 1800 to 1899

The Commissioners reported that, out of a total Llanfair Clydogau population of 471 persons, none attended day schools and none attended church Sunday schools, but that 120, attended dissenting Sunday schools operated by Capel Mair. The parish was one of only 20 within Cardiganshire without a day school. It was poor, isolated and had no facilities. Yet inadequate though this may have been, at least efforts were being made by the leaders of Capel Mair to make some provision for some of the people via its Sunday School work.

Making observations about education, social behaviour, the economy, the Welsh language and people's morality was a major aspect of the authors of the Blue Books. The written comments they received, principally from Establishment figures, were cited as "evidence". A paper submitted by the Reverend Llewellin, Vicar of Lampeter stated:

"The people derive a wonderful degree of Biblical knowledge from their habit of questioning each other in Sunday Schools. They are grossly ignorant of secular knowledge. Farm girls will answer questions on doctrinal points in their Sunday schools, such as on hardness of heart, original sin, etc, and be grossly ignorant of every other subject, but also grossly immoral".

Another paper published within the Blue Books by a well known local man was submitted by Thomas Williams, Clerk to the Magistrates in Lampeter. He wrote:

"The labouring classes are very poor here, and I have no doubt are too poor to afford sufficient instruction for themselves. There is a great deficiency in the means of instruction........The people are very anxious to obtain knowledge".

"I do not think the moral state of the people low; but for want of education they practice a great deal of low cunning. Generally speaking they are honest. Bastardy cases are however, very common. The women used to be ashamed of being in the family way, but are not so now; and promiscuous intercourse is carried out in a very great degree. I do not think that men and women generally sleep in the same room at farm houses; the men usually sleep in the hay loft but cases have occurred where women were got with child by farm servants whilst in bed with members of their own family. Better instruction would greatly improve this state of affairs."

A letter from John Rees, Tregaron Calvinist Minister, was included within the evidence. He wrote: "there is a great deficiency of schools for the poor in this neighbourhood.....There are few gentry in the neighbourhood and it is not likely that good schools will be established by them....There is a desire for better education among the parents of the poorer children here. Some better system of education is greatly wished for about here".

One of the Commission's staff wrote:

"The people in my district are almost universally poor. In some parts of it wages are probably lower than in any part of Great Britain.....The farmers themselves are very much impoverished, and live no better than English cottagers in prosperous agricultural counties."

"The cottages in which the people dwell are miserable in the extreme in nearly every part of the county of Cardiganshire".

Though, upon their publication, they were severely criticised for the comments they made on the Welsh people, the Blue Books written by the Education Commissioners, did provide much information about the poor standard of education within Wales at this time as well as the low numbers for whom such provision was made. The Books are also a valuable source of information about inadequate accommodation, facilities, books, teaching and the general economic poverty of Cardiganshire and many other areas in the country. A similar survey of many parts of England would also have revealed many equal inadequacies. For instance, Freidrich Engels[26] writing in 1844 about the Long Millgate area of Manchester said:

" Everywhere heaps of debris, refuse....passing among stakes and washing lines, one penetrates into the chaos of one storied one roomed huts in which there is no artificial floor; people living and sleeping all in one room" .

Slowly, in Wales, the Report did lead to an improvement in standards. For instance, the British and National Societies built 47 new schools between 1847-1870 in Cardiganshire, but none in Llanfair.

Llanfair School

Under the terms of the 1870 Education Act, there was a requirement for the setting up of elementary (5-12), education across the country. In areas where there was inadequate provision, School Boards were established on a parish basis. They could levy a charge on the poor rate of the parish. Events moved slowly in both the county and in Llanfair. Some 35 School Boards were set up in Cardiganshire between 1870 and 1880. On 25th November 1875, a School Board of five members was established for Llanfair parish and in 1877, Llanfair School was opened. It is understood that the funds for the new school were obtained from the Education Department in London. The Board adopted bye laws for its operation on 23rd November 1877[27]. The school was in a newly constructed building away from the physical centre of the parish, on the road leading from the church towards Glanrhyd and the mountain road to Llanddewi. This spot was chosen because of its close proximity to the location of a mass of small farm units on the edge of the mountains spread across the upper valley of the River Clywedog, where the majority of the children of the parish were living. Teaching was through the medium of English, yet the children were almost entirely Welsh speakers. Ceredigion Council website [28] states that "Welsh was not taught in established day schools until 1891, and since few people in rural areas spoke English, the Sunday Schools proved to be very popular. (for the

Chapter Five   1800 to 1899

retention of the use of Welsh). No Welsh was allowed in day schools and in many of them anyone caught speaking Welsh had the punishment of wearing a piece of wood hung round their neck bearing the words "Welsh Not". "Both teachers and parents thought this the most rapid way to advance the use of English for utilitarian reasons, but others saw it to be the most rapid way to stamp out the Welsh language".

A further improvement to the education system came in 1889 with the passing of the Welsh Intermediate Education Act. This led to the building of new schools for older children in Aberystwyth, Lampeter, Aberaeron, Tregaron and Cardigan.

The Log Book for Llanfair School[29] provides much information about social conditions within the parish and the efforts which were made to begin to persuade parents to send their children to school. It records the pressure upon the teacher(s) to deliver high quality education and shows the extreme importance given to the annual examinations, together with a yearly inspection. It is clear that, even in these early days, there was a link made between level of performance and the provision of grant aid for the running of the school. In July 1877, it was documented on the day of the annual inspection, that 82 children were present and "the scholars examined, many of them in the two lowest standards, passed a very fair examination in reading, writing and arithmetic. The following articles are required: maps; reading books; ball frame; log book; admission register. The girls ought to be taught sewing". By November of the same year, although there were 82 children on the admission register, a further 60 children were reported to the School Board as unregistered, and as such, not attending school. This figure is perhaps not surprising since parents had to make a payment as it was not a legal requirement for education across the country to be free, until 1891. Also, legal attendance up to the age of 10 was not made compulsory until 1880 for England and Wales.

Hence in October 1877 at Llanfair, parents were expected to pay 3d per week for the oldest children, 2d for others and 1d for the youngest. At the same time, a night school was started from 8.00 pm until 9.30 pm. The fees

Chapter Five   1800 to 1899

were a half penny per night. It must have been a daunting prospect for children and their parents to work out how to handle this new educational opportunity and challenge. Factors working against a straightforward launch of the new school would be firstly, a local population with no general expectation or experience of a school (except Sunday School); secondly, a requirement to pay, for those parents amongst a largely poor, rural population who needed to avail themselves of the new opportunities for their children; and thirdly, a potential loss of a child's labour in running the family farm if a decision was taken to enrol and pay the fee.

Despite these drawbacks however, in the pre Christmas period of 1877, the effort to get children into school was a great success in that, at the end of November, there were 102 on roll and by mid December, it had reached 123, "with more to come". As a result of this large increase there was a need for the selection and hiring of two pupil teachers.

The masters in charge of Llanfair school during the 19th century were:

- William James, 1877;
- Rowland Pritchard, 1877-1878;
- Daniel Jenkins, 1878-1897;
- Dr Cleaton Davies, 1897-1889;
- R. Satchwell, 1899-1901.

Dan Jenkins, yr hen athro, (the old teacher)

In mid January 1878, there was an outbreak of fever in the parish with three children dying, one who was on the school roll. Later in the same month "two boys from the school died, plus six others".

The growth in pupil numbers continued later in the year with 140 on the admission register at the end of February. But the complaint of the master in charge in March 1878, was that attendance was very low since some pupils were kept at home to help with harrowing. In June, the clash between attendance at school and the need to help with the family farm was serious in that the number present was again very low since, "they must watch the cows, whilst others are gathering wool on the mountains and turf making". The school master, Rowland Pritchard expressed his frustration with the Board for its inactivity in enforcing attendance. The clash between the requirement to attend school and the need to pay for education, must have been a major problem in these early years in the foundation of the school.

Concern about schooling versus farming remained a regular theme in the Log Book at this time. On 22nd July 1878, anxiety is expressed about the effect of the harvest upon attendance. On August 12th, the problem is the corn harvest and a whooping cough epidemic, when the attendance was only 31 pupils. By September, "the corn harvest was still not in from the top of the parish". In October, the attendance was low once more with "many children at home digging potatoes". In that month, a pupil from the school died of typhus fever.

Certificate of Merit. To David Pugh by Daniel Jenkins For regular attendance (424), 1880-1 Llanfair Clydogau Board School
(David Pugh lived at Pen Cilboa at this time and was about 8 years of age.)

Llanfair School circa 1890's. Daniel Jenkins on the right

Llanfair School circa 1890, Daniel Jenkins on the right.

The 1880 inspection report commented, "The school is in pretty good order and has passed a good examination in the elementary subjects." In January 1881, William Williams HMI, undertook a visit without notice. He called attention to problems in the playground, mental arithmetic and reading. The annual inspection in 1881 commented, "girls ought to be trained to sew more tidily".

The relationship with the family of the then major landowner of the parish is shown by the closure of the school for a day in October 1881 for the annual tea meeting which was held by Mrs Anne Jones of Glandenys.

1881 Aberdare Report on Education

At the time that Llanfair was still becoming established as a "Board School[30], concern was being expressed across Wales about the lack of sufficient Intermediate and Higher Education, hence the production of what became known as the Aberdare Report of 1881[30]. The report detailed and commented upon, what today we would call secondary and university education. With regard to the former, there was little provision for any youngsters in the country, the limited amount which was operational, was often very poor. In the general Llanfair area it was reported that the charitable Ystrad Meurig Grammar School had been founded for boys, in 1757. In 1881 it had 32 pupils in attendance. "The oldest 'boy' was 29 years of age and it appeared that it was not unusual for 20, or even 35 year olds to attend...most of the boys were the sons of farmers. Tuition fees of between three and six guineas were charged. Some 30 of the pupils were learning Greek and Latin, but natural science was not taught...significantly, the Welsh language did not feature in the curriculum".

Nearer to Llanfair was Lampeter Grammar School, re founded in 1805. In 1881 it had 17 pupils in attendance, of whom 12 were Anglicans. The fees were six guineas per annum. The Aberdare Report described the facilities in the school as being in a "wretched condition".

The general shortage of secondary school places was not addressed until the end of the 19th century, with the construction of secondary schools in Tregaron and Lampeter.

Llanfair Evening Continuation School.

In 1896 an initiative[31] got underway which had previously been tried for a short time in 1878, when a decision was taken to offer an "Evening Continuation School". This was first opened on October 19th 1896 with 26 students enrolled. By this time in the school's history, more older children were on the school roll, and this fact might well have encouraged the action. The master for these sessions was William Williams who instructed scholars in arithmetic, composition and writing. His records as evidenced in the additional Log Book associated with this venture, were meticulous in terms of numbers attending and standards of achievement within each session. His references on some occasions to poor attendance due to "excessively wet and boisterous weather conditions", give an insight into the circumstances in which these children would have attended these classes, often travelling long distances on foot in total darkness. It is clear that, whilst numbers peaked at 41 pupils attending at any one time, towards the turn of the century, they began to dwindle, with on some occasions, only two scholars attending. This is reflected in the reports by Mr. D. Evans from the Education Board, who appears to have inspected the Evening Continuation School on an annual basis. He wrote the following:-

Inspection report of 16th June 1897 – "This Evening School was ably and intelligently instructed and very satisfactory progress was accomplished during the past session."

Inspection report of 1898 -- "The instruction in the school is well and carefully given."

Inspection report of 1899 -- "The instruction is intelligently given. It is regretted that a larger number of young people of the district do not avail themselves of the opportunities for self improvement which this school places within their reach."

Chapter Five — 1800 to 1899

Daniel Jenkins : Llanfair School "teacher in charge" or headteacher

Daniel Jenkins, who lived from 1856-1946, was a distinguished "teacher in charge" or headteacher at Llanfair from 1878-1897, when he was appointed as headteacher at Llan y Crwys in Carmarthenshire. He was nationally renowned as an enthusiast of Welsh literature and music. His entry into the Welsh biography records describes him as very involved in the National Eisteddfod, in regard to which he was known as "Archdruid of the field". On the 1881 census he is shown as a lodger at Office Fawr. This was at a time prior to the building of the School House. In 1886 he married Elizabeth the daughter of William and Ann Williams of Llanfair[32].

John Thomas: famous photographer

John Thomas (1838-1905) was one of the pre-eminent photographers of people and scenes in Wales, during the 19th century. He was born in Llanfair (according to the census returns of 1841 and 1851) and as a boy, lived at Glan Rhyd, a house (now a ruin) located just off the Llanfair Road. His father was an agricultural labourer. According to the National Library of Wales biographical detail,[33] he moved to Liverpool in 1853 to work as a draper. With the development of photography he began to take photographs from about 1863. Upon his retirement he sold his collection of over 3,000 negatives to help illustrate the magazine Cymru. The collection is now in the National Library.

Church records

As previously stated, the church records fall into two categories, ad hoc notes on small pieces of paper from 1748-1813, and those kept in a more systematic form from 1813. Saving the former from destruction was a major task. We are indebted to the Llanfair vicar, Rev. Jonathan Evans for his decision in 1902, to take action to retrieve the rapidly deteriorating records and to re-write them. He said,[34] "by 1902 it was apparent that these records consisted of a heap of loose decaying sheets, so tender with damp and mildew owing to neglect in the early part of the 19th century, as to be well nigh useless. After careful manipulation, drying and arranging in order of date, a line by line and page by page transcription of the decaying originals was made". This considerable task took him 18 months. Without his endeavour, we would not have available to us today, the 1748 to 1813 records.

Burial records

The official book of records runs from 1813-1902. Where the burial had some unusual feature attached to it, the person making the burial entry has chosen to add a note to the simple recording of the event. The list below shows some of the more unusual entries:

- Sarah Morgans of Waun Wen, buried 10th May 1844, who was drowned;
- David Daniel of Penyrhyw, buried 9th March 1846, age 22, who was killed when "a wall fell on him";
- Margaret Jones of Carnau, buried 9th January 1847, aged 4 who "starved on the mountain";
- Henry William of Esgair Maen, buried 10th August 1872, aged 18, who was "killed by the lightning";
- Evan Jones of Llanfair Mine, buried 17th October 1884, who was "killed by a train".

Capel Mair

Capel Mair was founded in 1825. It is located on the opposite side of the river Teifi from St Mary's Church, close to Llanfair Bridge. Its origins lie in the actions of a small group of local people who had moved to Llanfair in 1790, and who had attended the Ebenezer Chapel (founded 1772), at

Chapter Five   1800 to 1899

Llangybi. Amongst them were Sarah and John Morgan, who moved to Pentre, a building which has now disappeared, but was then closer to the River Clywedog than the present Pentre. Religious worship occurred at their home until the death of Sarah in 1799. In 1806 her son John David Morgan and his wife Hannah came to live at Pentre. They too, were members of the Ebenezer Chapel in Llangybi. In order to make available, sufficient space for the Llanfair worshippers, the chapel members rented the old brewery in Llanfair. Speculation on the exact location of the brewery suggests it could well be close to Llanfair Bridge, in what the census of 1881 describes as, Llanfair Bridge Inn. (the present Bryn Heulog).

John David Morgan and Hannah Morgan later lived at Nantymedd, he dying in 1836 and she in 1873. Of their several children one, Rachel, upon marriage is believed to have lived at Caio in Carmarthenshire. She was baptised in 1808 in Llanfair and a photograph of her with her husband James Price taken in the 1870's is shown below.

Rachel Morgan

with her husband

James Price.

Chapter Five 1800 to 1899

Hannah Morgan was an important member of the Llanfair farming community for a number of years, continuing to run the present Nantymedd, with the assistance of family and servants. The farm is called Wernmedd on the 1841 Census and Gwernmedd in the Census of 1851, but by 1871 it had assumed its present name of Nantymedd. An indication of its size and economic importance can be gained from the number of people living and working there in 1851. Along with 64 year old Hannah, were four adult sons, one daughter and one grandson, plus two female servants, one male servant and a shepherd. As family members left home, their places in working the 191 acre farm were taken by paid employees, who came to live there. In 1871, along with 84 year old Hannah, were one son and a grandson, plus one shepherd, one dairy maid, two male farm servants and two female servants. All lived on the site. This is the same farm affected by the major fire of 1859, reported earlier.

In terms of the development of a new centre of worship in Llanfair, by 1824 it had become apparent that the rented brewery premises were not big enough to accommodate all the worshippers at the Independent Chapel, as the population within the parish was growing rapidly at this time. Hence, a decision was taken to obtain land, raise funds and construct a new purpose built chapel. In accordance with the law, people planning to set up an alternative place of worship to the Established Church, had to notify the Bishop and obtain a certificate. On 3rd October 1825, Evan Price, Gentleman, of Bwlchydwr in the parish of Kilcennin, wrote to the Bishop of St David's to "hereby certify, that a certain building, called and known by the name Llanfair Clydogau situated in the Parish of Llanfair Clydogau, is intended forthwith to be used as a place of religious worship by an Assembly or Congregation of Protestants". Issued on the same day was a certificate from the Registrar of the Court of the Bishop of St David's[35]. The main story of the development and operation of Capel Mair is contained in a book published in 1926 to commemorate 100 years of the chapel (1825-1925).[36] This book details as follows the formal setting up of Capel Mair:

Chapter Five — 1800 to 1899

"On November 29th 1925, Robert, Lord Carrington, and the under mentioned Trustees signed the agreement for the Capel Mair portion of ground, 32 yards x 24 yards.
Trustees:

Rev. Griffith Griffiths of Abermeurie, Llanddewi Brefi;
Thomas Griffiths of Blaencwm;
Thomas Richards of Penlantrawsgoed;
John Jones of Rallt;
David Pugh of Glanyrafon;
William Davies of Pentre;
John Morgans of Waunwen.

Second Trustees, chosen and appointed on August 21st 1868, at a meeting duly convened and held for that purpose by Rev. Thomas Thomas of Glannantcoy, Minister, Chairman:

Rev. Thomas Thomas, Glannantcoy;
Walter Griffiths, Blaencwm;
John Richards, Penlan;
Thomas Pugh, Glanyrafon;
John Morgans, Waunwen;
John Evans, Llanfair Bridge;
Evan Thomas, Llanfair-Fach;
John Thomas, Pantffynon".

The construction of the chapel cost £104.11s.10d and the work was undertaken by Thomas Williams of Pontrhydfendigaid. The bulk of this money, some £93.2s.10d, came from subscriptions and collections at Llanfair. The rest was given by Capel Erw in Cellan and Capels Noni, Ebenezer, Blaencyswch and Rhydybont. Bert Rawlins[37] points out that the religious revival of 1837 added over 100 new members to Capel Mair. Such was the demand for places in the chapel that a decision was taken to extend it in 1845. Key people involved in this were the Minister, the Rev. Stephens, along with Thomas Griffiths of Pentre and Thomas Richards of Pentrelan. The actions of 1845 saw the rebuilding of the chapel to double its original size.

Capel Mair (photograph 2008)

An indication of the significance of the chapel to the political and social life of the people is provided by a section in the book by Matthew Cragoe[38] entitled "Conscience or coercion? Clerical influence at the general election of 1868 in Wales". He wrote about the extent to which discussions within chapels may have influenced individual voting intentions. He says, "On the Sunday following the election, some members of the Independent Chapel at Llanfair Clydogau refused to take communion with those who had voted for the Conservatives. They believed them to be 'great sinners, hypocrites and traitors to the tenets and faith of their church', and demanded their excommunication".

Chapter Five — 1800 to 1899

1836 Tithe Commutation Act.

Under the terms of the 1836 Tithe Commutation Act (a replacement of the payment of tithes in kind with money payments), data was gathered across the whole of the country, and all areas were mapped during the period 1836-51, a map being produced for each tithe district. In the case of Llanfair, this was the parish. Accompanying each parish map, was an apportionment in the form of a table, with an entry for each map item by number. Each entry showed the owner of the land, the occupier, its name, area in terms of acres, rods and perches, rent charge payable and tithe recipient. This apportionment led to a "Provisional Agreement for the Commutation of Tithes", that for Llanfair is dated 16th October 1839[39].

A summary of the key tithe detail for Llanfair is shown below. The gross rent charge payable to the tithe owners in lieu of tithes was determined at £180 per year for the whole parish. The money was split evenly between the two tithe owners who were The Right Honourable Robert John, Lord Carrington and the Honourable George Laurence Vaughan. As an indication of how the system worked, David Walters at Park Neuadd had to pay a total of £4.17s.6d; William Davies at Pentre £8.12s.6d; John Walters at Llanfair Fawr £8.15s.0d and John Thomas at Oxen Hall 3s.3d.

Llanfair Clydogau Parish, tithe details of 16th October 1839					
LAND-OWNER	OCCUPIER	LANDS	QUANTITIES		
			A	R	P
Lord Carrington	Hannah Morgans	Nant Medd	297	0	12
Lord Carrington	John Morgans	Mill & land	2	1	32
Lord Carrington	Mary Williams	Cae Glas	89	0	27

Llanfair Clydogau Parish, tithe details (continued)

LAND-OWNER	OCCUPIER	LANDS	QUANTITIES		
			A	R	P
Lord Carrington	Mary Williams	Part of Tafarndy	7	3	11
Lord Carrington	Thomas Rees	Cefn foel Allt	68	3	19
Lord Carrington	John Evans	Clwt y patrwn	82	3	1
Lord Carrington	David Walters	Parc neuadd	295	0	34
Lord Carrington	William Davies	Pentre	558	2	18
Lord Carrington	Thomas Richards	Pentre lan	133	0	13
Lord Carrington	Thomas Griffiths	Blaen cwm	274	1	32
Lord Carrington	James Richards	Pen y lan	268	2	36
Lord Carrington	Morgan Williams	Gelli ddyfod	62	1	11
Lord Carringon	Morgan Williams	Lead & mine works	3	2	10
Lord Carrington	John Walters	Llanfair Fawr	456	2	21
Lord Carrington	John Morgans	Waun wen	219	1	21

Chapter Five — 1800 to 1899

Llanfair Clydogau Parish, tithe details (continued)					
LAND-OWNER	OCCUPIER	LANDS	QUANTITIES		
			A	R	P
Lord Carrington	David Jones	Mount Pleasant	2	3	7
Lord Carrington	David Jones	Esgair Maen	1	2	6
Lord Carrington	Griffiths Williams	Pant'r esgair	9	1	10
Lord Carrington	Richard Morgans	Dan'r esgair	4	0	13
Lord Carrington	John Williams	Blaen 'y bryn	12	0	20
Lord Carrington	John Jones	Ffos-las	21	3	4
Lord Carrington	Lord Carrington	Cefn' y bryn	8	3	38
Lord Carrington	Evan Thomas	Bryn maiog	6	3	9
Lord Carrington	Evan Thomas	Blaen wen	5	2	8

Chapter Five   1800 to 1899

Llanfair Clydogau Parish, tithe details (continued)					
LAND-OWNER	OCCUPIER	LANDS	QUANTITIES		
			A	R	P
Lord Carrington	Thomas Evans	Talwn glas	4	3	10
Lord Carrington	Evan Lloyd	Bryn glas	7	1	0
Lord Carrington	William Lloyd	Pant'y ffin	3	3	33
Lord Carrington	Henry Jones	Trebanne	7	2	1
Lord Carrington	David Evans	Ty waun	5	1	5
Lord Carrington	David Lloyd	Maes-glas	7	3	23
Lord Carrington	Joseph Pugh	Cwn croes	11	0	15
Lord Carrington	Thomas Richards	Cae Ysgwfa	1	1	13
Lord Carrington	Thomas Lloyd	Mountain Gate	0	3	11
Lord Carrrington	David Davies	Pencilboa	10	1	12

| Llanfair Clydogau Parish, tithe details   (continued) ||||||
| LAND-OWNER | OCCUPIER | LANDS | QUANTITIES |||
			A	R	P
Lord Carrington	Jenkin Jones	Bwlch'y ffin	3	0	19
Evan Davies	David Davies	Powell Hill	22	3	10
David Davies	David Davies	Wern Fawr	66	2	18
John Davies	John Hughes	Goitre'y allt	3	0	18
John Davies	David Morgan	Tir Bach	12	0	1
John Davies	Richard Morgans	Pen'y Graig	3	3	20
John Davies	Thomas Owens	Lluest	11	2	4
John Davies	Thomas Owens	Troed'y rhiw goch	3	0	2
Elizabeth Davies	Herself	Nant'y Clawdd	4	3	31

Llanfair Clydogau Parish, tithe details (continued)					
LAND-OWNER	OCCUPIER	LANDS	QUANTITIES		
			A	R	P
Joshua Davies	David Jones	Cwrt'y cylchau	12	3	25
David Daniel	Himself	Penrhiw	2	3	13
William Davies	John Thomas	Oxen Hall	7	3	12
David Davies	John Thomas	Blaen Pant	5	1	16
Matthew Davies	Margaret Williams	Hen Lluest y Bedw	1	3	30
David Evans	Margaret Williams	Llwyn Piod	3	0	9
Margaret Evans	Mary Williams	Gwar'y ffordd	4	1	12
Catherine Evans	Herself	Temple Bar	1	3	17
Mary Edmunds	Herself	Cwnc Sych	5	2	18

Llanfair Clydogau Parish, tithe details (continued)					
LAND-OWNER	OCCUPIER	LANDS	QUANTITIES		
			A	R	P
Thomas Griffiths	Himself	Cae garw	13	11	0
John Scandrett Harford	Rees Rees	Llwyn icir	9	30	0
John Scandrett Harford	Williams Rees	Llwyn Cnoy	64	1	21
-ditto-	David Thomas	Bwlch Gwynt	33	1	1
-ditto-	David Thomas	Llanfair Fach	164	2	22
-ditto-	Thomas Jones	Penlan-medd	143	1	20
-ditto-	William Rees	House/ Garden Fields	2	2	24
Rachel Hughes	Herself	Glan-rhyd	1	1	10

Chapter Five — 1800 to 1899

Llanfair Clydogau Parish, tithe details (continued)

LAND-OWNER	OCCUPIER	LANDS	QUANTITIES		
			A	R	P
John Jones (Trustees of)	John Davies	Goitre Fach	67	1	6
-ditto-	Evan James	Ffos Glai	17	2	16
-ditto-	David Owens	Fort Farm	28	3	10
-ditto-	William Morgans	Penlan Goitre	9	0	19
John Jones (Trustees of)	Timothy Jones	Llandulas uchaf	152	1	30
-ditto-	Rees Thomas	Pencae'r Odyn	39	1	0
-ditto- & David Davies	David Davies	Pen'y Garn	22	0	10
John Jenkins	Himself	Blaen Cyfswch	64	3	21

Chapter Five — 1800 to 1899

Llanfair Clydogau Parish, tithe details (continued)

LAND-OWNER	OCCUPIER	LANDS	QUANTITIES		
			A	R	P
John Jenkins	Himself	Glan yr Afon Cottage	1	0	5
John James	David James	Plas	2	2	30
David James	Himself	Cottage & Garden	0	1	10
Thomas Jones	Himself	Wind Castle	6	1	19
Morgan Jones	Himself	Ynys Moch	11	1	27
Benjamin Jones	Margaret Williams	Lluest y Bedw	10	0	39
John Jones	Himself	Llwyn yBedw	4	0	33
Evan Jenkins	Himself	Caban	2	0	8
David Morgans	David Lloyd	Pant y Nos	119	3	19

Chapter Five — 1800 to 1899

Llanfair Clydogau Parish, tithe details (continued)

LAND-OWNER	OCCUPIER	LANDS	QUANTITIES		
			A	R	P
Ann Marsden	David Davies	Cwm y Olchfa	3	0	39
David Morgans	David Evans	Beaulah	4	1	13
D Nicholl	Evan Evans	Part of Nant 'y Bwch	13	3	30
D Nicholl/David David Jones	David Jones	Part of Nant 'y Bwch	2	2	17
Thomas Owens	Himself	Cae Mynydd	3	2	0
Margaret Owens	Herself	Troed'y Rhiw Sarnau	8	0	8
Elizabeth Price	Ebenezer Thomas	Blaen Plwyf (part)	9	3	33
William Edward Powell	Joseph Williams	Cefn Moel Allt	35	1	27

Llanfair Clydogau Parish, tithe details (continued)

LAND-OWNER	OCCUPIER	LANDS	QUANTITIES		
			A	R	P
William Edward Powell	Thomas Davies	Blaen-wern	405	1	2
-ditto-	John Davies	Llwyn Felig	28	1	13
-ditto-/ Thomas David/ Davis Bowen	Thomas Davies	Gwaith-grof	1	3	2
Joseph Pugh	Thomas Pugh	Glan yr Afon (part)	1	2	7
Thomas Pugh	Himself	Glan yr Afon	13	3	5
David Rees	Himself	Troed-y-bryn	2	1	19
David Rees	Himself	Pant-y-fedwen	18	2	8
John Richards	Himself	Hendre-bant	9	0	10
David Thomas	John Williams	Ochr'y Bryn	6	3	10

Llanfair Clydogau Parish, tithe details (continued)						
LAND-OWNER	OCCUPIER	LANDS	QUANTITIES		
			A	R	P
Mary Williams	Herself	Bwlch'y Rhiw	5	1	4
John Williams	Himself	Pen'y-bryn	2	0	4

Religious Census of 1851

Another illuminating published document which gives information on the parish was the 1851 "Religious Census of Returns Relating to Wales: Vol 1 South Wales"[40]. This details information about both the Parish Church and Capel Mair. Significantly, the detail for Llanfair Clydogau shows the great importance amongst the local population of the newer Capel Mair. The statistics show 243 out of a total parish population of 588 attending either church or chapel.

The entry is as follows:

"Llanfair Clydogau Parish.

Area: 4,815 acres. Population: 271 males; 317 females; total

"LLANFAIRCLYDOGE PARISH CHURCH
Endowed: land £95; tithe £4; fees £1.
Space: free 120.

Chapter Five   1800 to 1899

Present: morning, 63.
Remarks: service morning and evening alternatively.
Morgan Williams Incumbent.
Lewis: perpetual curacy, endowed with £800 royal bounty; net income £63; patrons and impropriators, Lord Carrington and Captain George Laurence Vaughan; tithes commuted for £180.

C & C: 1 service in Welsh performed by the incumbent.
I & C: resident.

CAPEL MAIR, LLANFAIR CLYDOGE. INDEPENDENTS
Erected: 1825.
Space: free 42; other 228.
Present: afternoon, 135 + 45 scholars.
Average: general congregation 140; scholars 55.
David Stephens Independent Minister".

The disparity in parishioner attendance between the church and the chapel is indicative of the considerable growth in attendance at non conformist or dissenter churches/chapels throughout Wales. Llanfair's experience was repeated throughout the country and is a major feature of the 1851 religious census. In addition, in terms of local features particular to Llanfair, it may well be also suggestive of a continuing problem with both the physical state of the church building, or an overall problem with the day to day operation of the church within the parish. The situation with St Mary's as an operational parish church seems particularly bad, whilst that with Capel Mair was very buoyant at this time.

In 1859 Capel Mair welcomed 100 new members and in 1873, a further 60. People came from far and wide across this large and very dispersed parish. They would have been on foot and as a result, travelling times were long and the route was often difficult and arduous, especially for those journeying from many of the newer smallholdings on the mid and higher

Chapter Five   1800 to 1899

slopes of the eastern uplands, the detail of which is shown so clearly in the tithe information of 1839. In 1862, in order to cater for the demand and to reduce journey times to services, a decision was taken to build Maesglas school house, just off Sarn Helen, close to the present Maesglas house. Prayer meetings were held regularly, with services on one Sunday each month. In addition, there was a successful Sunday school held there. Whilst this boom in attendances and public support was taking place, a catastrophe was engulfing the nearby St Mary's Church.

The gaoling of the vicar and his "visitation of God"

We have a fascinating insight into the condition of the Llanfair parish from archive papers[41] concerning the curacy (position of vicar), and of the difficult ten years leading up 1859. In a sad, personally tragic and highly embarrassing situation, Morgan Williams, the incumbent of both Llanfair Clydogau and Llangybi parishes, died on 1st December 1859 in Cardigan Gaol, where he had been held for 23 weeks as a prisoner of debt. He was 57 years of age. He was buried in St Mary's Churchyard, Cardigan on the 3rd of December and the record of his burial in the church records states, "Morgan Williams, abode, Cardigan County Gaol (Incumbent of Llanfair Clydogau and Llangybi in the County of Cardigan)". His death was also registered with the Official Registrar on 3rd December. This record confirms death in the County Gaol, that he was a priest and that the registration of death had been undertaken, not by any family member, but by the Coroner for Cardiganshire, who had held an inquest on that date. Oddly and incredibly the cause of death was described as a, "visitation of God"!

Quite how an officially appointed Coroner can hold an inquest on the same day as the death, and then attest to death as being as a result of a "visitation of God" seems beyond comprehension by today's standards. One wonders what scientific evidence he had for his diagnosis. Lest we think the Coroner was making a moral statement about the unfortunate Morgan Williams, it needs to be borne in mind that coroners of the time, frequently had no legal or medical training and often declared death to be a "visitation of God" if actual cause of death was not apparent.

In keeping with the etiquette of the time, since a vicar was a major Establishment figure, it is not surprising that there was also a newspaper announcement of his death, though its precise location was carefully concealed. The *Welshman* newspaper of 9th December 1859, reported within its death announcements, "On the 1st instant at Cardigan, after a long illness, the Rev. Morgan Williams of Henllan Court near Lampeter and Llanfair and Llangybi Churches, Cardiganshire, aged 58". Note the lack of clarity between the Cardigan church records and the newspaper, over whether he was in fact 57 or 58 years of age. A further lack of clarity is provided by the death announcements column in the *Carmarthen Journal,* which printed on 9th December 1859, "Williams-on 30th instant, the Rev. Morgan Williams of Llanfair, Cardiganshire." Since these newspaper statements had to be formally placed and paid for, the differences in regard to the date of death is odd. The placement also suggests someone, perhaps a family member keen to do the right thing by announcing to the public, the death of a church minister. Ministers were both well known and important in terms of the Establishment, and also within the 19th century, in terms of society. Yet, we do not know who placed the death notice, for there is a degree of mystery surrounding his life and personal circumstances.

Since a death in gaol of a minister of the Established Church was unusual, and the reasons for his being there seem curious, a substantial research effort has been mounted to try to shed light on the case. This endeavour has also tried to ascertain how the events leading up to his gaoling affected both Llanfair and his spiritual and pastoral role in the community. The research has taken in the National Archives in London, archives at the National Library of Wales, Ceredigion and Carmarthenshire Archives, Lampeter University archives, parish records and newspaper files.

Newspapers seemed a possibly good starting point, but the locally orientated *Cambrian News* did not start publication until later. However the weekly *Welshman,* the *Cambrian* and *Carmarthen Journal* were all

Chapter Five 1800 to 1899

published from the early 19th century, focusing mainly upon areas to the south of the country, but reporting some events from Cardiganshire, especially sittings of the Quarter Sessions in Cardigan and meetings of some clubs and societies. The summary of meetings of the Quarter Sessions does not help in seeking detail about Morgan Williams' case, for as he was in gaol for debt, his case would not have reached the Quarter Sessions since there, the focus was upon criminal rather than civil cases. In fact from 1846, the main vehicle for civil matters of dispute was the newly created County Courts, which from 1850, were able to deal with cases with a value of £50 attached. Yet, their records don't help provide information either, since Morgan Williams' debt was well in excess of this amount, at over £300. Hence, the route way to claim damages and seek redress against such an alleged debtor was through the Westminster court system of the Queen's Bench or something similar, such as the Court of Exchequer of Plea of Westminster.

Efforts to seek information about the vicar and gain a local perception of his situation from the Llanfair church "annual vestry" minutes also fail, since they, along with those for the other perpetual curacy of Llangybi which he also held, no longer exist with regard to most of the 19th century. These minutes might have given some inkling of the events happening to him and the state of the parish in terms of issues or problems at this time. Nevertheless, in spite of difficulties in sourcing the facts, detail gleaned from a large number of places, including diocesan records and London court details, enables the following account to be written.

Morgan Williams: early years and appointment to Llanfair

Morgan Williams was born in about 1802 in the parish of Gwnws, (located between the rivers Ystwyth and Teifi, north of Tregaron). He was the son of Edward and Jane Williams. The family were farmers of 100 acres of land at Nantbyr Uchaf. He was fortunate in living close to the Ystrad Meurig Grammar School, which had two advantages, firstly he could attend

Chapter Five   1800 to 1899

---

a school, and secondly he could attend an institution with teaching beyond what might be called elementary education. His parents must have been keen to further his development and secure opportunities for his betterment and would have paid an annual fee for his education. It was a small school with a limited curriculum, but with important links to the Anglican Church, and thus provided an early educational route for the recruitment of a number of clergy throughout the 19th century. They were mainly young men who came from homes where their parents were tenant farmers who were keen to further the education and opportunities of their sons.

He took the opportunity presented to him by the establishment of the new St David's College, Lampeter and enrolled there as a student. According to the archives at the College, the first ever year group of students started on 1st March 1827 and he joined this small group on the 8th March of that year, with records showing him as being 24 years of age. Unfortunately, all did not go well with his studies and new life in Lampeter away from his home at Gwnws to the north, and he left the College in midsummer of 1828. (the records do not state why). However, he returned once again to St. David's as a student in February 1830, clearly being determined to persevere with his studies. Yet, his difficulties with his life at St David's continued and he was rusticated (sent down), for the period of the Lent term in 1831. Why he was punished in this way is unknown. After completing his rustication he returned to St David's yet again, but once more he encountered problems in that he was "rejected" at the midsummer examination in 1832. Why he had failed again, and what happened next, is unclear, but his name is not shown in a list of those receiving a licence in divinity at the College.

In spite of this setback he secured appointment at some point in time, as firstly a deacon, and then secondly, a priest within St David's diocese. The evidence for this is provided by Crockford's Clerical Directory, published many years later and covering the period 1859/60. His own self certified entry states:

Chapter Five   1800 to 1899

" Morgan Williams, Llanfair Clydogau, Lampeter, Cardiganshire-
St David's College, Lampeter; Deacon 1833; Priest 1834, both by Bishop of St David's."

What precisely he did in the years immediately after leaving St David's in about 1832 is unknown. But Llanfair church records show him working in some sort of support or relief capacity at the parish church in 1836. Morgan Williams is shown as "Officiating Minister" at a number of burials, baptisms and marriages in Llanfair from November 1836, instead of the salaried incumbent, Rev. David Williams. He assisted his namesake for a number of years. Surprisingly, from 1836 until his official appointment as the curate, he was the minister at 37 out of 41 funeral services which took place at the church. He also undertook most of the baptisms and marriages over the same period. The church records give no guide as to his substantive job at that time, or as to what the parish's own priest was doing.

In the 1841 census, at about the age of 39, Morgan Williams is shown as living on the High Street in Lampeter and is described as a clergyman. But where was he largely working, besides assisting the Llanfair vicar? St David's Diocese records show he was appointed Perpetual Curate of Llanfair on 26th February 1842, on the nomination of the Honourable George Vaughan. He was one of the two men, Lord Carrington being the other, in whose gift the religious "living" lay. The two Patrons appointed the minister alternatively, and it was Mr Vaughan's turn. The living of Llanfair Clydogau had an annual income of £67, whilst Llangybi produced £66, at this time.

He took over the two parishes after the death of the previous incumbent David Williams, who had been in post from 1792 to 1842. Testimonials supporting his actual appointment as incumbent, dated March 1842, were signed by the Rector of Llanddewy Velfry and the Vicars of both Lampeter and Kerry, who all confirmed they had personally known him for the last three years. As there was no vicarage in Llanfair or Llangybi at this time, it is unclear where he went to live upon his appointment.

Chapter Five 1800 to 1899

Morgan Williams: his business and financial activities

A most curious and surprising clue to his possible living arrangements, allied to his interest in business, comes from the 1839 tithe apportionment documentation for Llanfair parish, which lists him as the "occupier" of two properties, both owned by Lord Carrington. These were, a house and farm Gelli Ddyfod (62 acres), and the Llanfair Mine and Works (3 acres).

But why was he occupying a farm and a lead and silver mine with its works, and at which of the two closely linked properties was he living? It should be remembered that at this time, the vicar's income for the church was quite reasonable. In fact, it was large by comparison with the broad mass of the population. The incumbent of a perpetual curacy was no longer the poverty stricken member of the Establishment of earlier centuries.

Adding to his seemingly complex mixed ecclesiastical and entrepreneurial relationship, Morgan Williams took another eventful decision in June 1849. He approached David Jones and Company, bankers of Carmarthenshire, and arranged to borrow £300. In accordance with the procedure of the time, he signed a promissory note committing him to pay back this money, with interest (at quite a high rate of return), upon demand. Surprisingly, after a relatively short period, some six months later in December, the bank demanded repayment of the loan, which with interest then totalled £320. Upon his failure to pay, David Jones and Company, which consisted of brothers David, William and John Jones, quickly undertook legal action in the Queen's Bench[42] at Westminster to seek recovery. On 7th January 1850, Morgan Williams was reported in court records as being, "unable to deny the action against him," and the court concluded that, with the bankers' costs for bringing the action, he owed £336.10s. But why did he borrow the £300 at a very high rate of interest in the first place? Why did the bank demand repayment after only six months of the loan operating? Also, why, with an annual salary from his benefices as a curate of £133, was he not able, or prepared to make any payment of the loan?

Chapter Five   1800 to 1899

This court decision was rapidly followed by the issuing of a writ[43] on behalf of David Jones and Company, from the Queen's Bench in January of that year for, "the whole and interest on £335 from 7th January 1850, besides all expenses of sequestration and levy". The money demanded related to damages which they claimed they had sustained (which were unspecified), as well as the Rev. Williams, "not performing certain promises and undertakings". The agent acting for the Messrs. Jones later reported to the court that Morgan Williams "had no goods or chattels or any lay fee in his balliwick" whereby he could pay the damages awarded. One wonders what happened to his belongings and salary. As a result, the bankers applied for, and convinced the court to issue, a writ against the Bishop of St David's for recovery of the money, since the parishes of Llanfair and Llangybi were both in his diocese.

This seemingly unusual approach towards obtaining ones dues was very regularly used in the 19th century with regard to clergy of the St David's Diocese. So relatively matter of fact was it that the diocese created a specific administrative system to deal with claims and writs. A large record book titled: "Letters of Sequestration for Debt[44] was established. In the book over the period 1836-1895 there are recorded several dozen cases whereby a claimant had been before one of the courts in Westminster, usually the Queen's Bench, to firstly seek a writ for a sum of money owed by an Anglican minister in the diocese, and then secondly to seek a writ against the Bishop for collection of the amount owed. The process in the diocese was for the Bishop to then appoint a sequestrator to try to obtain the money from his defaulting clergyman. The detail of the writs outlined in the Sequestration Book are for amounts ranging from £700, to smaller figures such as £35, £40 or £54. The process developed to collect this money was standardised within the diocese in that a general pro forma letter was devised and printed. Gaps were left for the insertion of the case particulars and the form, once completed, was sent to the chosen sequestrator. In the case of Morgan Williams, with the arrival of the writ from the Queen's Bench, approved by Thomas, Lord Denman, the Bishop appointed David Morgan of

Chapter Five   1800 to 1899

Lampeter in February 1850, as his Special Sequestrator to, " take, seize, collect, and receive into your hands, possession and safe custody all manner of rents, revenues issues, profits, tithes, commodities, duties, pensions, portions, sum and sums of money, and all other dues and emoluments, whatsoever appertaining or belonging to the perpetual curacy and parish church of Llanfair Clydogau and Llangybi", in order to secure payment.

One would think that, upon being aware of the writ against him and the involvement of the Bishop, plus the appointment of a well known Lampeter man as sequestrator, Morgan Williams would have been disturbed and anxious to put things right as quickly as possible. Nevertheless, no early progress was made in dealing with this financial embarrassment. He made no payments to either the sequestrator or the bankers. Equally, the sequestrator did not seize his assets or divert his income from the Queen Anne's Bounty Glebe lands. Surprisingly, attempts to recover the money from him were still proceeding in 1855. In that year the Bishop had to appoint a new Sequestrator of Morgan Williams' assets, William Jones of Lampeter, after the death of his first appointee. (This seems to be the same William Jones of David Jones and Company, bankers, who later was to become the major landowner of Llanfair and who lived at Glan Denys). The debt, in spite of Morgan Williams' steady and continuing salary from his two livings at Llanfair and Llangybi, was still £335 plus interest in November of that year, nearly six years after the original writ was issued. The new sequestration document was issued after a further application of the bankers to the court in Westminster.

It is understood that efforts were made to try to recoup the loan from 1855 through until 1859. It is unclear who took the legal action which saw Morgan Williams gaoled in the summer of 1859. It is thought likely to have involved the actions of a London court since there was no reporting in the Welsh newspapers referred to above. The initiation of legal action could have been either David Jones and Company or the sequestrator acting for the St David's Diocese. Evidence shows that Morgan Williams had made some

Chapter Five   1800 to 1899

payments by the time of his gaoling. In his own statement in his letter quoted below, it seems that he had managed, belatedly, to make payment of some of his debt. He wrote of owing only £160 at the time he was in gaol in the July of 1859

Morgan Williams: his personal and family circumstances

To add further to the mystery of the activities of Morgan Williams, in the early part of 1850, he is described in the court records as resident at Nantbyr, Gwnws, his parents' home. This location, bearing in mind the bad condition of Cardiganshire roads, would have made for a difficulty in administering to the needs of his two lots of parishioners and the two parishes to the south. The March 1851 Census shows him in a new and perhaps more straightforward location, this time at the Rectory in Cellan, where he was described as "a lodger".

Attempts to discover and research more about Morgan Williams' background have unearthed a marriage announcement in the *Carmarthen Journal* of July 1851 which reads as follows: "On the 11th inst. at Llanfair Church, Cardiganshire, by the Rev. Evan Johnes Evans, the Rev. Morgan Williams to Elizabeth, only daughter of the late John Joshua Esq. in the county of Cardigan". So he appears to have married. Yet did he, and was this him? Checking the facts should be simple, but they are once more shrouded in a degree of mystery. The Llanfair church records of marriages do not record such a marriage and in fact unusually, only record one marriage taking place in 1851 and that is not of Morgan Williams. In addition, there is no marriage entry for him at Llangybi church. Also no evidence of a marriage of Morgan Williams can be found from the records of the official Registrar of births, deaths and marriages, but then it was not a legal necessity to register a marriage until 1875. Nevertheless, the circumstantial evidence tends to support the likelihood of the accuracy of the newspaper's wedding announcement. Firstly, in regard to the alleged minister administrating the marriage ceremony, there were in fact two men called the

Chapter Five　　　　　　　　　　　　　　　　　　　1800 to 1899

Rev. Evan Evans in the nearby area in 1851, one at Trefilan, where he was curate and the other at Nantcwnlle where he was vicar. Secondly, a woman by the name of Elizabeth Joshua, named in the newspaper as his bride and aged 34, was living in Cellan (the parish where Morgan Williams was living four months before the wedding), with her widowed mother in 1851. Her father was called John, the same name as within the newspaper announcement. When he was alive the family had lived in Llanfair, where he was a tailor. Thirdly, Elizabeth was known personally to Morgan Williams since he officiated at the burial service of her father in Llanfair Church. Fourthly, in the 1850 Clergy List for England and Wales, there is only one Rev. Morgan Williams living in Cardiganshire. Hence, all the evidence around the marriage announcement appears to relate to the Llanfair vicar and suggests his probable marriage at about 49 years of age.

If indeed he did marry, it was at a time when he had enormous personal pressure upon himself because of the writs issued against him and the Bishop's appointment of a sequestrator to claim some of his assets. This pressure must have caused him great anxiety, worry and embarrassment. As an Establishment figure with obvious connections with the rich and politically influential of the area, he is bound to have been a subject of gossip, debate and scrutiny. It is also inconceivable that his parishioners would not have known something of his clash with both the bankers David Jones and Co. and the Bishop through his sequestration order.

So, throughout the 1850's we have one of the most senior Establishment figures in Llanfair parish, the subject of personal discussion and scrutiny by a local public, found lacking in dealing with his finances, guilty of serious debt and being pursued not only by his Bishop, but also by a local sequestrator. One must imagine that the pressures upon him had a serious and undermining effect upon his capacity to carry out his religious and pastoral duties. How did his congregation view him and how was he seen by the wider population within the parish? How did he function in undertaking his church services?

In the 1850's, in addition to the serious issue of his debt, Morgan Williams was also involved in correspondence with the Diocese on a number of occasions about his living arrangements. In 1857 and up until 1858 he had to "petition for a license for non residence" because neither of his parishes had a house available for him. This arrangement was agreed by the Bishop's representative. This must have left an impression upon him about church procedures and protocol because on 20th August 1859 from gaol, he wrote to the St David's Diocese to request the necessary license to be, once more, non resident. (because he was in goal). As well as sending him the necessary neatly designed two forms to fill in, the diocesan administrator wrote to the man in gaol, "I perceive you are a non resident incumbent without a license and non resident. I trust you will lose no time in rectifying this error".[45] Quite how he would do this from Cardigan gaol is an interesting speculation.

Overall, the 1850's were years of pressure, stress and personal difficulty for Morgan Williams as he wrestled with issues of his debt. We know nothing of his matrimonial circumstances, but assuming he did marry Elizabeth, where did they live and was she the person who placed his death notices in the newspapers? Evidence quoted below shows his two parishes as encountering severe operational problems and hardship at this time. Falling attendances at church, a failure to maintain the church buildings, the lack of a school and an enormous growth in attendance numbers at the rival Capel Mair, all became apparent to Establishment observers in the area. Put simply, the problems with the parish seem to have been widely known, and some of the reasons were linked to him.

Morgan Williams: dealing with his imprisonment

In terms of his imprisonment and his efforts to get released, a number of letters from the St. David's diocesan records about his situation are quoted below. Fascinatingly, a letter he wrote on 14th July 1859 from gaol in the early days of his detention, is available. He sent this to the Rev. Thomas

Chapter Five   1800 to 1899

Walters, a vicar working near Narbeth in Pembrokeshire and who was a native of Llanfair. The Rev. Walters' mother was the sister of Thomas Griffiths of Pentre within the parish. This letter outlined his financial and legal plight and asked for assistance in clearing his debt of between £150 and £160, "before I can come out". If the amount is correct then it indicates that he must have paid off some of his debt, since at the beginning he owed at least £335. He provided an indication as to why he was in trouble when he wrote:

"The mine was the ruin of me. I worked it myself for a long time but I have nothing to do with it now, only receiving the Royalty". This is presumably the Llanfair mine or mines referred to above and operated by Jonathan Marsden until 1837, the same mine as he is shown as occupying in the 1839 tithe apportionment records. It is unclear what he means when he says he worked it himself. His reference to "working" the mine suggests a business endeavour and probably means he was the proprietor, leasing the site and putting in place a manager to operate the mine on his behalf. It is likely that he was responsible for operational costs in terms of driving the workings deeper underground as more lead and silver was sought, along with the paying of workers' wages. The detail of the start up of the lead mine in the 1750's by Thomas Johnes, with extracts from his letters to his brother quoted earlier, show how difficult and frustrating operating a mine could be. Similar difficulties and cash requirements could well have faced Morgan Williams.

The Rev. Griffiths Thomas of Cardigan, who had visited him in gaol, learned some details of the reasons for the imprisonment. In December 1859 he wrote to the Patron of the Llanfair Church, Lord Carrington, to say:

"His creditors behaved very cruelly towards him in not giving him time to settle his affairs, for it was in his power to do so if time had been granted to him. He was in a very indifferent state of health when he entered prison. I paid great attention to him during all the time he was in prison, consequently he became so attached to me that he desired to be buried in my churchyard at Cardigan and was buried here on Saturday last".

Had his creditors behaved badly towards him? In fact, they had been seeking repayment of their loan since December 1849, and had been unsuccessful in getting a full reimbursement.

Conditions in prison in general would have been very hard and primitive. Detail from Cardiganshire Quarter Sessions records show typical meals for male prisoners in the main part of the gaol as being a breakfast of oatmeal gruel with bread, and a dinner of soup with bread or perhaps augmented by a little meat and potatoes.[46] However for debtors, conditions were better than those which generally applied. Coincidentally, a meeting of the Cardiganshire Quarter Sessions in 1859 on 5th April discussed and agreed revised gaol conditions for debtors. The meeting decided:

"They may, when not receiving any allowance from the prison, receive from their friends or purchase, food or clothing, but no debtor should be allowed to receive or purchase more than one pint of wine or one quart of beer or cider in any one day of 24 hours. Articles of food or clothing should only be received between the hours of eight in the forenoon and four in the afternoon".

" They should be permitted to work and follow their respective trades.... provided their employment does not interfere with the good government of the prison". "They should attend divine service when performed" The Prison Chaplain reported "divine service and a service in English and Welsh had been delivered every Sunday and those able to read were in the habit of reading the Bible and other religious books every day".

The same meeting restated that the various forms of debtors included:

Chapter Five   1800 to 1899

" Debtors committed for bankruptcy, for frauds under the bankruptcy laws and debtors remanded for frauds by insolvency debtor courts, should be subject to the same rules as debtors committed under other laws".

At the July 1859 Quarter Sessions[47] the keeper of the prison at Cardigan made his report. He said there were 10 prisoners, comprising three debtors, five convicted felons and two uncommitted felons. One of the three debtors was presumably Morgan Williams.

It was not until 10 years later in 1869 that debt was decriminalised and as a result, routine imprisonment for debt ceased, other than in cases of fraud or a deliberate refusal to pay. The issue of imprisonment for debt was clearly an important one in the first half of the 19th century. For instance, Charles Dickens' father was imprisoned for debt which had a severe impact upon the family and was a major influence on the author's future writing.

In an attempt to secure his release from gaol Morgan Williams suggested a way forward in his letter to the Rev. Walters. He wrote:

" I must pay £150 to £160 before I can come out and now if you can get me £200 I shall resign the valuable livings of Llanfairclydogau and Llangybi to the Patron, the Right Honourable Lord Carrington. I do not expect you to give your money away without sufficient security-so you must get a promise from the Patron...tell him you are the same as John Walters" (one of his well known Llanfair relatives). He urges the Rev. Walters to go first of all to one of his Lordship's solicitors, Mr. Freshfield or Mr. Newman, in order to be taken on to meet Lord Carrington. He suggests that the Rev. Walters gets Mr. Newman to write out what Morgan Williams needs to do next, and that he will then resign after signing a document in front of a witness within the gaol. After this has been done he asserts, "then you can legally pay me £200",
since you will be "paying me for my life interest in the living" in the light of your discussion with Lord Carrington. He also reminds the Rev. Walters that, in approaching Lord Carrington, he should remind his Lordship of his family relationship link to Thomas Griffiths of Pentre "who pays rent

annually" to his Lordship and also "that a great many parishioners are your near relatives".

Morgan Williams goes on to explain the value of the living:

"The living is worth a full £250 a year....it is now considered the best of the livings in the neighbourhood. I receive from the mine work that is on the Glebe land, £30 or £40 very often".

"I leave you to do things....to your own way, but it must be done quick and as soon as possible". (letter M Williams, Cardigan Gaol 14th July 1859).

It is unclear from the correspondence what action the Rev. Walters was able to take. The implication from the letter was that the he should try to raise the money to clear the debt so that the gaoled curate could then resign his living but that at the same time, he should point out to Lord Carrington, his role in helping to solve the problem and remind him of his close family connections with the parish in the hope of being appointed to the created vacancy. Whatever the proposed plan was, tragically the Rev. Williams was still in gaol when he died in December 1859. It seems likely no agreement to provide him with £200 was forthcoming. He did not resign.

A further insight that this was indeed the case is provided by the Rev. Thomas Walters' letter to Lord Carrington of 12th December 1859. It does not refer to any agreement with Morgan Williams with regard to him taking over the parish. Instead, it points out to his Lordship that his uncle, John Walters of Llanfair, "often promised to do what he could for me in the case of a vacancy, but since he is no more, I hope your Lordship will give me the livings". He points out that most of his relatives are in the parish and that, "many of my ancestors lie in the churchyard of Llanfair." Urging his appointment he writes, "I have a great wish to get these livings and would sacrifice anything almost to procure them".

Chapter Five　　　　　　　　　　　　　　　　　　1800 to 1899

Understanding why the living was so financially attractive lies in examining the structure of the vicar's annual income. There were two major components, rent monies from tenants he had on the Glebe lands which went with the parish, and a payment from the tithes. The Glebe lands were located in four neighbouring parishes, but not Llanfair. The income they generated would be dependent upon their farming potential, as well as whether any mining company wanted to enter into a lease to explore and mine the land. There was nothing unusual in clergy seeking to take such commercial opportunities as presented themselves with the lead mining companies. Permission to lease out the Glebe in this way involved asking for the consent of both the Patron and the Ecclesiastical Commissioners in London. Surprisingly, in 1859 just prior to his gaoling and untimely death, Morgan Williams was involved in trying to negotiate a lease for mining under the Glebe at Llechwedd Hen, Llanbadarn Fawr near Aberystwyth, with the Bronfloyd Mining Company. Once again he was involved in a commercial enterprise. Perhaps he was trying to raise money to pay off his debt. However, this seems to be only a reference to his latest venture and was not the reason for his imprisonment.

Though Morgan Williams' death was reported in two South Wales newspapers, we are no clearer as to details of his personal family and whether he did in fact have a wife called Elizabeth. His grave in the churchyard of St Mary's Cardigan has no headstone and hence there is no monumental inscription to consult for family information. Census information for the family home at Nantbyr suggests he had two brothers and a sister. Someone placed and paid for the newspaper announcements of his death.

The scramble to appoint a vicar in 1859/60

As is apparent from the Rev. Walters' letter, Morgan Williams' death opened up a scramble from other members of the clergy to secure appointment to the Perpetual Curacy of Llanfair and Llangybi. A number of the application letters have survived in the St David's diocese records in the

Chapter Five 1800 to 1899

National Library. They provide a powerful insight into the workings of the ecclesiastical system at the time and the crucial pivotal role played by the Patron, Lord Carrington.

In his application the Rev. Morgan from Bala said, "these two parishes, as you well know have been neglected for years". The Rev. William Evans from Silian (the eventual successful applicant), wrote saying, "I can say that if appointed I would endeavour with all my power to raise the condition of the two parishes morally, intellectually and physically......I should also do my best to provide in each parish, good schools and school buildings". The Rev. Roger Williams, curate of Lampeter wrote, "Your Lordship is probably aware of the neglected state of these parishes-having no schools and the fabrics of the churches (especially Llanfair) are in rather a bad condition. If I am appointed to the living, it shall be my prompt and earnest endeavour to meet the wants of the neighbourhood by repairing the churches and establishing schools". The Rev. Charles Lloyd of Betws Bledrws, writing in support of another person's application said, "the parishes are much neglected by the late unfortunate incumbent and the result is that dissent is very strong in both parishes". In January of 1860 he took services in the parishes and wrote to Lord Carrington to say he was "much pained at finding such a miserable small congregation at both places". Henry Davies of Beaumaris wrote to say, "I am in every way qualified to take charge of the parish of Llanfair Clydogau which is now, I am sorry to say, in a most ruinous state". Another vicar wrote pointing out why he was a good candidate for the job and that amongst his most positive features was the fact that he did not drink, smoke nor take snuff. Mr Inglis Jones of Derry Ormond (a major landowner in the area), wrote to state that the two parishes had been very neglected for a number of years and that parishioners felt completely abandoned.

In summary, these contemporary letters provide an insight into the state of the Llanfair parish from the viewpoint of a number of Anglican clergymen. Neglect, abandonment, the lack of a school and in general a poor overall condition morally, intellectually and physically was said to characterise life there. Spiritually too, for the Anglicans there were serious problems with the growing number of dissenters in the parish. We have already noted that Capel Mair recorded an enormous surge in membership in 1859 in that they gained 100 new members. Some of these could well have been former members of St Mary's church. Others were simply parishioners who were choosing their most comfortable home for religious worship to be the independent Capel Mair. In addition to these serious issues, the church building was in need of repair. Overall, as one clergyman put it, the situation in Llanfair was "ruinous".

The power of Lord Carrington

We would consider surprising today, the amount of power over the appointment that accrued to the Patron, Lord Carrington. He was Robert John Carrington, second Baron Carrington (1796-1868), variously owner of large estates in Buckinghamshire and Cardiganshire and a Member of Parliament. He acquired his Llanfair estate from his father, the first Baron Carrington who had purchased the lands in the early 19th century. All applicants wrote to him at his address in Whitehall, London, addressing him as "My Lord". One wrote in a most obsequious and ingratiating manner, "Therefore, as the two livings are now vacant, and in your Lordship's gift, I would feel extremely obliged and thankful to your Lordship, if your Lordship would be pleased to grant the said perpetual curacies to my nephew ". Other Cardiganshire gentry and landowners became involved in the appointment. Lady Llanower of Abercarn sent a personal testimonial on behalf of one applicant, whilst, the Rev. William Evans wrote, "My Lord, I have had the honour of waiting on the Countess of Lisburne yesterday morning and she mentioned that she had been kind enough to write to your Lordship about six weeks ago to recommend me......My neighbour and parishioner Mr William Jones, the Banker at Lampeter, desires me to make use of his name". In December 1859, the Earl of Lisburne from Crosswood wrote to Lord Carrington to ask that he "give Llanfair and Llangybi to my friend Mr. Evans,

I should be most obliged". Later a testimonial was received from his wife, the Countess. Upon the appointment of the successful candidate, the Rev. Evans in January 1860, the Countess wrote to thank Lord Carrington. She stated: "I am very glad that my man was found worthy. I thank you kindly for giving him Llanfair and am most grateful to you for being so good as to listen to my wishes...My interest in him arises from his having married a daughter from one of our tenants who taught me Welsh and asked me to recommend him".

1860: the Glebe

As we have seen, the new vicar of Llanfair and Llangybi, William Evans, formerly of Silian, inherited a situation in which negotiations had been taking place with Bronfloyd Mining[49] to lease an area of the parish's Glebe land at Llechwedd Hen at Llanbadarn Fawr. This general area was a major lead and silver mining centre within Cardiganshire, but which declined greatly in the 1880's as the profitable ores were extinguished. Upon taking over the living he wrote to the Ecclesiastical Commissioners asking for agreement to a lease of 21 years for 44 acres of ground. The Royalty to be paid by the mining company was to be one fourteenth part of the value of the minerals worked. There was also to be a lease for the company to "take the waterpower on the site for a payment of £10 per annum, to be paid to the Rector"[50]. Yet, though the £10 for water power was initially paid, the mining company appears to have not made any Royalty payments in respect to the value of minerals worked. In 1873 the Ecclesiastical Commissioners placed the matter in the hands of a legal firm in order to " take such steps in the matters as they may deem expedient for the protection of the interests of the living". This approach was not successful and in 1878 the Ecclesiastical Commissioners noted that the affairs of the mining company had been "thrown into confusion by the defalcation of the Managing Director-criminal proceedings were taken against him and resulted in a sentence of imprisonment". I have seen the annual statistical returns of the Ecclesiastical

Commissioners in relation to this lease and they show nil returns for revenue from mineral workings throughout the 1880's, 1890's and through to 1911. A report by a geological engineer expressed the view that there was very little lead within the ore which was mined.

The Bronfloyd Mining Company was a very new company in 1859. The *Carmarthen Journal*[51] of February 1859 reported upon its 3rd Annual General Meeting held in London. The Company publicised very positive news stories for its shareholders and the media about high quality ores and the size of lodes. These encouraging and positive news stories did not accord with the later difficulties in finding lead or the problems in making the agreed payments to the Ecclesiastical Commissioners on behalf of the Llanfair Minister.

Development of the railway

As part of the railway building boom in the 19th century, Parliament approved in 1860, a scheme for the construction of a railway from Manchester to Milford Haven, via Llangurig and Llanidloes. Prior to the route being determined and funding obtained for initial construction, the *Carmarthen Journal* [52] reported in 1860 of an important local meeting, held at Cellan, which was attended by Thomas Griffiths of Pentre, plus "other gentlemen, freeholders and farmers. Some of them bought shares in the company" and there was a favourable response to the scheme. Building did not get under way until 1864 and then only to begin laying the route from Pencader towards Pontrhydfendigaid. Overall, the Manchester to Milford Haven Railway was never finished. Driving a route to Llangurig would have been an enormous and costly engineering feat. Instead the eventual line ran from Carmarthen to Aberystwyth, with a branch to Aberaeron. The route touched the western edge of the Llanfair parish. Stations were built at Lampeter, Derry Ormond, Llangybi, Pont Llanio and Tregaron. The line allowed easier access to Llanfair and was a contributory factor in assisting the dairy farming industry in the Teifi valley to switch away from the production of butter, to the supply of fresh milk which could be transported away to markets in the industrial areas of South Wales in the later years of the century,. The single line railway was closed down in 1965, whilst the route to Aberaeron survived for a few more years. Economically, the railway company always struggled to raise enough initial construction capital and in addition, operational levels of passengers and freight were never high. The line would have helped improve communication for Llanfair residents.

Lord Carrington's sale of lands

In 1868 the 2nd Lord Carrington died and he was succeeded by Charles Robert Wynn Carrington, the 3rd Baron Carrington. The evidence suggests that a decision was taken by the new landowner to sell either all, or some of his Cardiganshire lands. A public auction was held in December 1868. The lands and properties were placed into a series of lots and various people made successful bids.

Purchase of Llanfair lands by William Jones of Glandenys

An indenture[53] of 24th December 1868 shows William Jones being the highest bidder and purchaser of "the Manor lands and various heredits" which were the first 18 lots in the auction. He paid £35,900. Within the auction he also acquired the right to appoint alternatively "in perpetuity to the vicarages of Llanfair Clydogau and Llangybi". He may well have bought other lots additional to the first 18 lots outside this specific indenture. It seems clear that he did acquire other Llanfair lands from their owners over the following several years. When the Glandenys Estate was sold in 1930, the number of properties put up for auction was large and indicated an extensive property portfolio extending over an area of several parishes.

Chapter Five — 1800 to 1899

Rebuilding St Mary's Church

Sometime in the early years of the 19th century, efforts were made to improve the physical state of the Llanfair church. However, we know from the comments from the applicants for the vacant curacy, that the church building was still unsatisfactory in 1860. Confirmation of some of the adverse comments about the state of the church building in Llanfair is provided by an account in a publication of 1861[54] dealing with various churches which had undergone "restoration". The author writes:

"The church of Llanfair Clydogau was visited by us that morning. We remembered it some years ago before it had been "repaired"; and fortunately some notes of it had then been taken; on the present occasion we found it, not restored-the word will not apply-we had rather use the common phrase of "done up" in the cheapest and ugliest manner that any building could experience. This church as it stood a few years ago, though humble, preserved traces of 15th century work and was capable of restoration in consonance with its original character at small cost. It is now "done up" in the commonest meeting house style, with bad windows and is altogether despoiled of every architectural feature".

There was an acute awareness amongst the small number of parishioners of the problems with the church building. Working with the new enthusiastic incumbent of 1860, Rev. William Evans, efforts began to be made to raise sufficient funds to repair and renovate the church building. This took a long time. However, 26 years later, on 6th May 1886 at a parishioners' meeting (Vestry), the 17 people present approved plans drawn up by J.H. Middleton, H.A. Prothero and G.H. Philpott, architects of Westminster, Cheltenham and Newport. The resolution which they passed is shown below.

"At a Vestry held in the Parish Church of Llanfair Clydogau, in the County of Cardigan, pursuant to public notice in writing, affixed on the door of the said church, on Thursday the 6th May 1886, for the purpose of taking into consideration the propriety and necessity of repairing and restoring the said Parish Church, it was proposed by Mr Henry Morgan of Tan yr Esgair, Churchwarden, and seconded by Mr David Williams, Blaenywen, that the said Parish Church, which is in a dilapidated condition, be restored by voluntary contributions according to the plans and specifications prepared by Middleton and Co, Architects of Cheltenham. The said places and specifications having been considered and approved of, it was agreed and resolved by the undersigned inhabitants and parishioners to repair and restore the said church as proposed by the said Churchwarden, Mr Henry Morgan, and it was also agreed and resolved that a "faculty" should be applied for in order to commence and proceed with the necessary work."

Signatories:

William Evans, Vicar of this parish;
Henry Morgan, Churchwarden;
David Williams, Blaenywen, Farmer;
David Pugh, Churchwarden;
William Williams, Pentre, Farmer;
David Richard, Penlan, farmer;
David ...., Wenaullt, farmer;
Thomas Griffiths, Penlan Medd, farmer;
David Jones, Waunwen, farmer;
Stephen Davies, Pantyesgair, farmer;
Evan A Davies, Llanfair Fawr, farmer;
Richard Rickaw;
Timothy Davies, Lluest, farmer;
William Evans, Office Fawr;
David Jones, Mill;
Jane Davies, Cnwcsych;
William Davies, Gellyddyfod" (St David's Diocese Faculty records)[55].

Estimates for the work were £1,000 and at the date of approving the plan, the parishioners held only £700 in the National Provincial Bank in Lampeter. This considerable sum of money had been raised by the parishioners themselves. In order to secure approval for the scheme from the St David's Diocese Faculty Board, on 27th July 1886, a financial bond had to be put into place. This was for £2,000 in the name of the Rev. William Evans and Walter Davies. The tender specification documents show a new vestry to be constructed, along with a new church floor, roof, pews and windows, plus a complete repointing of all the existing stone work. Completed quotations for the work were to be returned to the Rev. Evans at Llangybi with building work expected to take eight months. The existing records do not show what

St. Mary's Church (photograph 1980's)

the contract price was, or which company undertook the building work. Kelly's Directory[56] gives the cost as £1,225 (1895).

In anticipation of the church building being out of commission during the construction work, steps were taken to enable the church to function temporarily elsewhere. In 1886 the St David's Diocese received a formal application to award a licence for the Llanfair Primary School Room to be able to be used for solemnizing marriages and for it to be consecrated for the holding of divine services. These applications were granted.

Once the scheme for renovating the church was approved, the work got underway and was concluded in 1888. By that time, the population within the parish was continuing its decline, as it did steadily and remorselessly until the period after 1971. It fell from 614 in 1861 to 512 in 1891.

Another gazetteer of the late 19th century was Horsfall Turner[57]. He refers to the new St. Mary's building and that "many bits of 15th century workmanship disappeared from the church in restoration, but the ancient font was able to be returned". He mentions the old church being thatched, of which we are aware because of the notes of the Easter Vestry meetings. He concludes by stating that, "The prosperity of Llanvair was somewhat greater in the days of working of the lead and silver mines, but like many others of the great Plynlimon syncline, these mines are now abandoned and inundated".

Parish poor and the Poor Law

Horsfall Turner, in his writing quoted above, suggests that Llanfair's prosperity had declined during the 19th century. In terms of the provision for the poorest, destitute and most needy members of society, major changes took place during this time. Firstly, the 1834 Poor Law Amendment Act was passed and became operational. This changed the whole basis under which the Poor Law operated. Secondly, unions of parishes took place for the delivery of the Poor Law. Thirdly, gradually workhouses were built. The Lampeter Union was formed on 15th May 1837, one of five for the county at that time. Boards of Guardians were set up to administer poor relief and govern the workhouse. The workhouse for the Lampeter Union was not

Chapter Five   1800 to 1899

constructed until 1876 hence until that time, all relief for paupers had to be outdoor. Even with its arrival, in keeping with the practice throughout the whole of Cardiganshire, most people classified as being in financial need continued to receive outdoor, rather than indoor relief. As indicated above, references to paupers in burials ended at St Mary's in the 18th century. However, harshness of language and with it stigmatisation, continued. Baptismal records for Llanfair throughout the 18th and 19th centuries show that when a child had no legally recognised father, the method of recording the baptism was to show within the records, the mother's name and alongside the insertion, the words in the 18th century of "bastard" and in the 19th century "illegitimate".

An indication of the application of the Poor Law and of its operation in society within Llanfair parish, is provided by the case of John Morgan[58] of Felinfawr, Llanfair. He was born in 1816 and lived with his parents, who were tenants of Lord Carrington, at the Llanfair Mill, before taking over the Mill himself. He stated that, "when I took over the mill it had only one pair of stones for grinding purposes, but there was plenty of water power there to drive three pairs of mill stones. As there was a good deal of work for corn mills in the neighbourhood and many of the country mills were not going in the summer for want of water, I went to the expense of purchasing and fixing two additional pairs of grinding stones, which cost me £200". He paid an annual rental for the Mill tenancy of £25. The work was undertaken in 1865 and he claimed it became the best mill in the neighbourhood. He asserted that in 1868, Lord Carrington sold his Llanfair Estate, including the Mill to William Jones of Glandenys, but that he did not receive any compensation to cover him for the investment he had made in the property. He alleged before a Commission of Inquiry into land in Wales, that his failure to get compensation preyed on his mind, "and in consequence my health was undermined. I had to give up my work and abandon the Mill. I also lost my hearing, and for many years had to break stones on the road in order to earn my livelihood. My health got worse. I had to give up stone breaking, and apply for parochial relief. I now (1894), receive from the Guardians of the

Lampeter Union, 3s. 6d per week towards maintaining myself and my wife, who is also old and infirm and thus, unable to assist me. We brought up nine children and I paid rates to the parish of Llanfair for many years". This statement was made before the members of the Royal Commission on Land in Wales and Monmouthshire, meeting in the Town Hall at Lampeter. Mr. Morgan was living at this time at Park Powell, within the parish. The case became a cause célèbre and was reported in newspapers such as the Westminster Gazette and the Pall Mall Gazette of 1894, with an emphasis upon Mr. Morgan investing his scarce resources, but receiving no compensation upon subsequent sale, from a rich peer of the realm.

Sunday Schools

One of the important developments during the 19th century was the creation and operation of Sunday Schools. These provided an opportunity for youngsters to receive religious instruction, meet other similarly aged young people away from the home and have some experience of being read to by an adult. They may also have allowed some instruction in reading. Some of these features were especially important during the period prior to the introduction of compulsory education for all, the first stage of which only happened in Llanfair in 1877. The role of the Sunday School was clearly regarded as important by the Welsh Educational Commissioners in their survey of 1847. They reported that 120 Llanfair children attended a Sunday School operated by Capel Mair, but that there was no similar church facility.

Such was the demand for Sunday Schools in the area, that the various churches and chapels in Llanfair and surrounding parishes began to decide that the best solution was to construct a special Sunday School building. Ideally, this should be located some distance away from the main place of worship. It would then overcome the necessity for children to walk such long distances to church or chapel.

Chapter Five   1800 to 1899

Those built in the 19th century included the following:

- A building on the mountain plateau at 1200 feet between Esgair Garn and Brynmeinog in Llanddewi Brefi parish;
- Ysgoldy Gogoyan in Llanddewi Brefi parish;
- A building at a height of 900 feet on the hills near Pant-y-pistyll in the upper part of Cellan parish;
- Ysgoldy Mynydd, belonging to St Mary's Church, in Llanfair parish, just east of the Clywedog Ganol, north of Glan Rhyd;
- Maes Glas, belonging to Capel Mair, just north east of Sarn Helen, near the present Maes Glas house.

Some of the detail concerning the development of Maes Glas is contained in the centenary book about Capel Mair.[59] It shows the involvement of six church ministers in the initiative and records the development as follows:

" A lease of a small portion of ground, 12 yards x 10 yards, was obtained on January 18th 1865 from David Lloyd of Maes Glas, Llanfair, for a term of 999 years at 6d a year rent by the following Ministers:

Rev. Thomas Thomas, Cellan Court, Cellan;
Rev. Henry Jones, Ffaldybrenin;
Rev. David Davies of the Town of Lampeter;
Rev. Benjamin Phillips, Tynygwndwn;
Rev. Thomas Jones of Temple Bar, Ystrad;
Rev. William Evans of Aberayron.

The Trustees were:

William Lloyd of Waunmacwydd;
William Lloyd of Pantyffin;

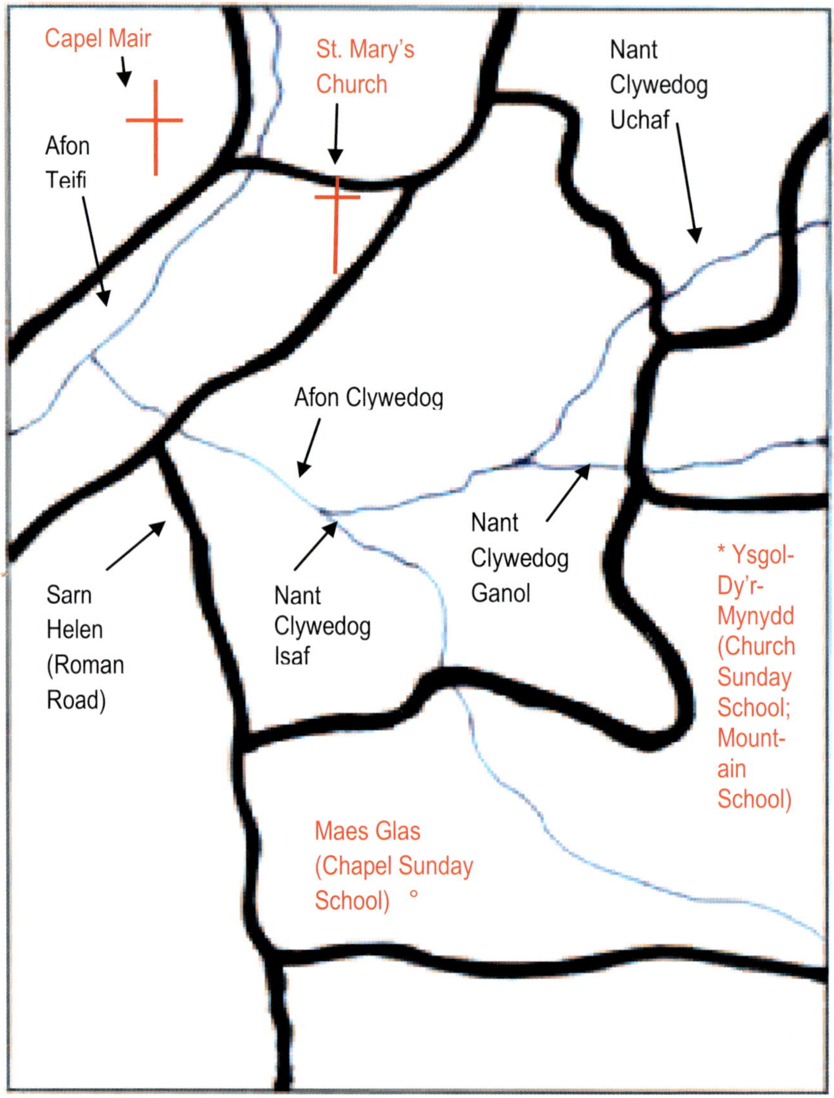

Chapter Five 1800 to 1899

Map labels:
- Capel Mair
- Afon Teifi
- St. Mary's Church
- Nant Clywedog Uchaf
- Afon Clywedog
- Nant Clywedog Ganol
- Sarn Helen (Roman Road)
- Nant Clywedog Isaf
- * Ysgol-Dy'r-Mynydd (Church Sunday School; Mountain School)
- Maes Glas (Chapel Sunday School) °

Llanfair's Sunday Schools in the 19th century (not drawn to scale)

Chapter Five   1800 to 1899

John Jones of Moelfryn;
Benjamin Lloyd of Panteg.

> As witnesses".

It was reported that 60-70 attended Sunday School at Maes Glas in the 19th century.

Servants and farming in the 19th century

Scrutiny of the census returns from 1841-1901 gives a very detailed insight into the structure of both the economy and society of Llanfair. Firstly, most of the larger farms employed workers who were normally referred to within the census returns as servants. Secondly, these workers, both male and female often lived on the farm. Examples of four farms, two from each side of the Teifi, are shown below for 1881. In that year:

- Llanfair Fach had living on the farm, two male farm servants and three domestic servants;
- Nantymedd had living on the farm, one indoor servant, one male farm servant, one boy and two female domestic servants;
- Llanfair Fawr had living on the farm, two female domestic servants;
- Blaen cwm had living on the farm, one male indoor farm servant, one dairymaid and one female domestic servant.

These large numbers of employees are a further explanation for the relatively high Llanfair population during the 19th century. As machinery began to be used to a greater extent in the 20th century, the demand for labour in the form of farm workers declined considerably. This restructuring is a further reason for the sharp reduction in the parish population which is described in the next chapter.

The parish between 1900 and 2008

> Victoria (until 1901); Edward VII (king 1901-10);
> George V (king 1911-36); Edward VIII (king 1936);
> George VI (king 1936-52); Elizabeth II (queen 1952-).
>
> **Significant developments**
>
> 1902 Boer War ends; 1909 Old Age Pensions start for over 70's;
> 1914-18 1st World War; 1927 BBC; 1936 BBC television;
> 1939-45 2nd World War; 1946 National Insurance expanded;
> 1948 National Health Service; 1955 ITV starts; development of motorways; expansion of secondary and university education; Nov. 1982 start of S4C.

In the book "Highways and Byways in South Wales[1] A.G. Bradley, in 1903 provides an account of the parish. He wrote:

"A new church at Llanfair Clydogau stands upon an ancient site. Beneath it are vaults in which the Johnes family are buried to this day. Just across the lane is a quiet unnoticeable farmhouse, and near it, the workings of a deserted lead mine. The latter, for years employed much labour, the former contains the scant remains of a country seat of famous stocks. It has all vanished now save an outhouse, but it is said the walls were 15 feet thick and carried the date of 1088 upon them! Be that as it may, a particular favourite of Charles 1, a Lloyd once lived here, who was member for the county and resigned his seat when Stafford fell. The Johnes of Havod succeeded to it later and altogether it was a notable mansion, once surrounded by a deer park of several hundred acres. Not a trace of its former glories now survives".

Chapter Six   1900 to 2008

Though the "glories" of a former age of the Johnes, the Lord Lieutenants, the gentry and the lead mines may indeed have gone, the parish throughout the 20th century was far from static or stagnant. Change in the structure of society continued to occur and much more of the written evidence of this has survived than in any previous century.

Llanfair population statistics

Year	Population
1901	441
1911	406
1921	380
1931	293
1951	324
1961	212
1971	187
2008 est.	240 estimate

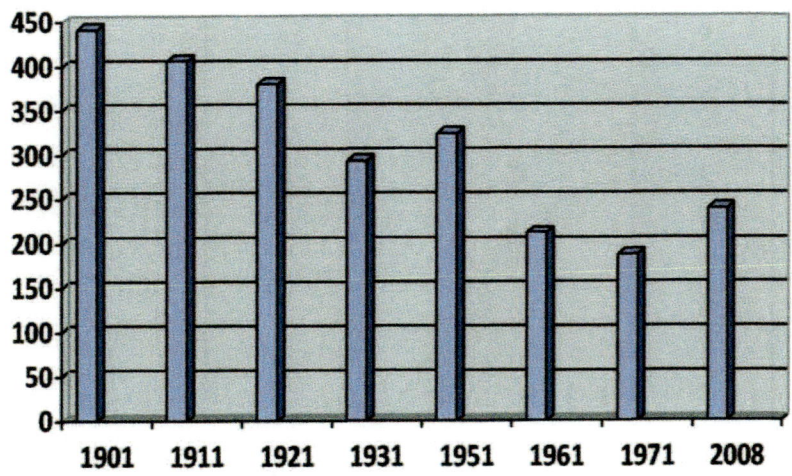

Chapter Six   1900 to 2008

A great deal of structural change took place in Llanfair, and in Cardiganshire in general throughout the 20th century. In the parish the population continued its steady downwards decline from 441 in 1901 to 187 in 1971. In percentage terms this is a considerable reduction of 57%. Precise parish population figures are more difficult to ascertain from this date, following the amalgamation of Llanfair parish with Cellan for local government purposes in May 1987 and the creation of a joint Community Council. However, in 2008 there were 202 electors in Llanfair and there is today, an estimated population of 240 people. Agriculture, the largest employer of labour throughout the history of the parish experienced a considerable decline in terms of number of separate farms or smallholdings throughout this century. A number of the smallest family units were abandoned and people moved away.

Yet, in spite of the population contraction, the parish continued to be a vigorous and enterprising place. Social progress took place with the arrival

Llanfair celebration in the early 20th century

of a piped mains water supply and sewerage system to the lowland areas adjacent to the Teifi. Most of the properties away from the valley bottom on the east, still do not have these facilities and instead, use private water and drainage facilities. Electricity arrived in 1950 in areas close to the River Teifi.

Chapter Six   1900 to 2008

Mountain roads were improved and surfaced with tarmac. Both the church and chapel continued to operate successfully, and during the earlier years of the century, ran Sunday Schools in buildings they owned on the eastern uplands.

Above, Coronation Prize Group of Llanfair Ladies

To the right, Capel Mair Sunday School class (teacher: Mary Lloyd)

Llanfair School.

During the 20th century the headteachers were as follows:

- Hugh Hughes, 1901 - 1917;
- M J Thomas, 1917 - 30th April, 1935;
- Jack Poole, 3rd June, 1935 - 1943;
- Eiddwen James, 6th December 1943 - 31st August 1975;
- Jean Davies, 1st September 1975 - April 1976 (last Log Book entry).

A Llanfair social event in the early 20th century

Llanfair gathering, 1900's (Evan Evans of Esgair Maen on the left)

Chapter Six　　　　　　　　　　　　　　　　　　　　　　　1900 to 2008

Family at Glanrhyd, note the haystack to the right

Women gathered at Llanfair Fawr, 1927

Chapter Six   1900 to 2008

Throughout the century the school continued to provide a vital service for the children of Llanfair. Information from its Log Book provides much detail about the social and economic operation of the parish. Life was hard for the children and their parents. Many of the children had to travel two to three miles on foot, to get to school, from the dozens of small scattered farmsteads dotted across "Llanfair Mountain". They often had to travel along the many footpaths which criss-crossed the hillsides before joining a non metalled road or track. Their journeys sometimes took them over footbridges which had been built across the steams. Fewer children came from the western side of the Teifi since there were lower numbers of farmsteads and houses there.

An Education Office commentary[2] of 1911, seeking to explain low attendance levels at Llanfair, brings out some of the difficulties. The commentary states that out of some 40-50 children on the school roll during the year:

- Not more than seven children of school age reside within one mile of the school;
- Roads the children have to travel down to school are in winter, like mountain torrents, which greatly affects the attendance of younger children;
- The district being entirely agricultural, the gathering of stores and the getting in of hay, corn and potato crops, affect the attendance of the older children.

Examples I have selected, from the Log Book[3] to illustrate the facts behind these points include the following entries from the headteacher:

- " Weather is favourable for good attendance, but the farmers are busy bringing in a store of peat from the mountainside for winter use" (4th October 1912);

- "Terrible thunderstorm. All the footbridges over the Clywedog were swept away and the roads were roaring torrents" (11th June 1915);
- "This spell of fine weather has brought the attendance to a vanishing point" (30th July 1914);
- "No school on Monday, hiring fair at Lampeter, so a holiday given" (12th November 1920).

The impact of a wave of ill health, bad weather or the demands of the farm at home can variously be seen from the statistics on attendance. On one date in 1918, out of a total roll of 40, only eight were in attendance because of heavy rain. In December 1927, out of a roll of 55 children, only 25 attended because of the cold weather and illness.

Reports of the external inspections of the school were generally good in commenting on standards and conditions. However, the report by an HMI (Her Majesty's Inspector), of January 1922, expressed concern about the three teachers who lived in Lampeter and cycled to work at the school. "It is feared that they feel tired occasionally by the time they reach Llanfair".

Health issues are reflected in the Log. In November 1910 there was an outbreak of diphtheria which killed one pupil and saw the district Medical Officer order the closure of the school for three weeks. In February 1911 there was an outbreak of whooping cough with serious consequences for a large number of children and attendance plummeted. So bad was the diphtheria outbreak of 1910-11 that four children died suddenly of the disease.

Information from the Syllabus Record and Report Book dated 31st August 1911 provides the following detail. The school, which was divided into the Lower and Upper Division, offered the following syllabus:-

English   - Reading; Composition; Penmanship and Spelling.
Welsh   - Reading; Translation and Composition.
Recitation in English and Welsh.
Arithmetic - Written and Oral.

Chapter Six 1900 to 2008

Geography/History.
Observation Lessons/Nature Study – of surroundings, natural features, industries and plant life.
Moral Instruction – hygiene and temperance.
Physical Education – rules of public health, food, drink, cleanliness, air and clothing.
Gardening – for boys.   Needlework for girls.
Drawing and Music.

The Lampeter area School Board papers[4] constitute another source of information about the school, which was referred to as "School 56". One note shows a closure of the school on public health grounds from March 5th 1931 until March 11th 1931 due to an outbreak of influenza. Other papers list a series of inspection reports, both on the progress of the pupil teacher and on the standards achieved by the school pupils. A report of 1902 refers to "the condition of the school being gradually improved by the new Master, who deserves credit for the progress made so far, but the state of the children's attainments was so unsatisfactory when he took charge that much remains to be done before work reaches the standard necessary to win the higher Principal Grant...". However at this time, although the school appears to have fallen short with regard to the teaching of the more academic subjects such as handwriting, mental arithmetic, history and geography, for standards in singing, drawing, needlework and agriculture, it attracted favourable reporting. The 1902 Report also gives comments upon the conditions within the school as follows: "The appearance of the floor and of the stove and its surroundings is very untidy. Habits of neatness cannot be properly cultivated as long as it is allowed to remain in its present condition. The ventilation of both rooms should engage the serious attention of the School Board. The classroom is too crowded with desks and gallery. The removal of the latter and the substitution of a level floor, furnished with desks, calculated to promote a healthy position of the body is very desirable."

Chapter Six   1900 to 2008

Minutes of monthly meetings of the Education Board which took place in Lampeter, document the resignations and appointments of staff to the school and details of applications for pay rises made by various members of staff. For example, Miss Gertrude Hughes was appointed as Assistant Mistress on March 3rd 1905 on a salary of £25 per annum, but this sum was subsequently raised to £30 per annum, with a claim for payment of arrears from her, due to her commitment to the teaching of sewing. Other matters dealt with by the Board at these monthly meetings included dealing with the payment of invoices from the school for stationery purchases, improvements to the fabric of the building such as a new pump for the urinals and a new cloakroom for the infants, along with provision of goods such as a desk for the Assistant Mistress and manure for the school garden. It was also within the remit of those attending these meetings to consider how to deal with those parents who persistently failed to ensure that their children attended school on a regular basis.

Before secondary education was introduced for all Cardiganshire children, Llanfair Board School operated as an "all age" school, retaining the bulk of the children through until the school leaving age. The exceptions were a small number each year who were put forward for a selection examination, and if deemed clever enough, were allocated a place at a secondary school in one of the nearby small towns. An example of how this operated is provided by the case of Jano Jones, the mother of Beti Davies of Bryn Castell[5]. She was born in 1912, lived at Hendrebant in Llanfair and attended Llanfair School. When she was 11 years old she was allocated a place at the selective secondary school in Tregaron, and in the 1920's, was a pupil there. Such was the difficulty of travelling the eight miles to school that she had to board in Tregaron, Monday to Friday. Travel to and from school was accomplished by her walking each Monday morning, carrying her personal belongings and school equipment. This sounds like a very daunting and challenging task for a young pupil.

Another example of the early travel away from Llanfair is provided by the case of Tom Thomas[6] formerly of Gwarffordd, and now Salisbury. He

Chapter Six   1900 to 2008

---

described life in the 1930's when pupils were allowed to sit entrance exams to both the County School at Tregaron and St David's Grammar School in Lampeter. If successful at both exams, a pupil could chose the one they preferred. He says that Gethyn Jenkins, Ben Lloyd-Jones and himself all chose the Grammar School. As the Education Department only provided a bus to carry pupils to the County School and not the Grammar School, they cycled each day for six years. He wrote: "Many a day we rode three abreast and completely ignored the coach horn blaring at us". They fixed newspapers next to their skins when it was raining. He makes clear the great difficulty the Grammar School boys from Llanfair faced in having very little knowledge of the English language. He has also drawn attention to the fact that many of his fellow students joined the Armed Forces in 1938 and 1939 as there was little work available locally. Several were killed, including Ben Lloyd-Jones who is named below.

Several photographs of the whole of Llanfair School are shown below. One of the earliest shows 56 pupils, whilst that for 1955, shows 26. In 1971 there were 17 present for the photograph. There was great pride in the school and parish when in August 1946, Eiddwen James, headteacher was invited by the government to join only four others from across Wales at an International Teachers' Course at Dulwich College, London. Besides teaching, she was also an accomplished writer of poetry and had several books of her poems published.

As the numbers of children in the school began to decline, discussions took place with regard to its closure and the movement of the children to Llangybi. For instance the minutes of Parish Council of June 1974, show a reference to a question asked of the County Council about what will happen to the primary school building when it is closed. The Parish Council moved to thank and commemorate Eiddwen James upon her retirement. In June 1975, it was decided to collect for a testimonial for her in view of her forthcoming retirement after 32 years as school mistress. The presentation to her took place on 30th July in the Church Hall, with refreshments prepared by Llanfair WI and a cheque being given to her, along with a rose bowl

Chapter Six   1900 to 2008

Llanfair School circa 1926

inscribed in Welsh. The school continued to operate through until 1976 and the last entry in the Log Book is for 7th April of that year. The children on roll at the closure date transferred to Ysgol Y Dderi at Llangybi.

Llanfair School circa 1933

Llanfair School 1955

Llanfair School 1974

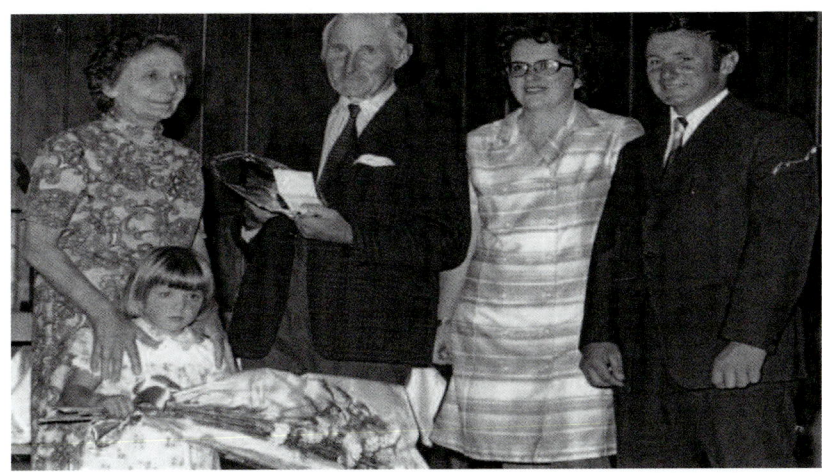

Retirement presentation to Eiddwen James, headteacher. Left to right : Eiddwen James; Dilys Evans (Nantymedd); W. Lloyd-Jones (Llanfair Fach); Gwyneth Evans (Llanfair Fawr); Ian Evans (Esgairmaen).

Chapter Six 1900 to 2008

The Valuation Office Survey, 1910-15[7].

Under the terms of the 1910 Finance Act, a survey was undertaken of the whole of England and Wales in order to record the extent of property holdings. The result for the Llanfair parish is summarised below. The actual sizes of land holdings are in acres, rods and perches, but for ease of handling this data, only the acres are shown.

Llanfair Clydogau Valuation Survey, 1910 - 1915			
Building/land	Acres	**Building/land**	Acres
Llanfair Fawr	233	Silvermine	
Dolau	22	Caeglas	32
Tynlone		Part of Caeglas	4
Refelbach		Caeglas Cottage	
Rhew		Tucking Mill	
Office Fawr+ Cae Sarah isaf	5	Part of Tafarndy	6
Pentre	235	Parcneuadd	177
Gellydyfod	58	Clwrt patrwn	119
Waunwen+ Mountain Pleasant	225	Blaen cwm	74
Penlan and Waunsaith-wyr	192	Hendrebant	9
Nant y medd	289	Llanfair Mill	8
Troed y rhiw		Allotments	11
Ty coch		Esgair Mine	6
Pen y garn	22	Wennallt Isaf	25
Cefn foelallt	53	Esgair Ddu	30
Allotment	6	Allotment	5
Pentrelan and Blaen Pant	78	Pentre Cottage	

Chapter Six — 1900 to 2008

Llanfair Clydogau Valuation Survey, 1910 - 1915			
Building/land	Acres	Building/land	Acres
Llanfair Bridge		Office Fach	
Llanfair Bridge Inn		Llanfair Estate (woodland)	53
Gwarffynnon and Llwynpiod	14	Llanfair Parish (tithes)	
Cae Squire	1	Tynewydd	
Glen View		Llaingoch	55
School House		Tynfron	13
Blaencyswch	65	Blaenwern	105
Great Western Railway	1	Part of Blaenwern	4
Llwycuar and Blaenplwyfr	74	Tancoed	3
Part of llywnieir	8	Pencaerodyn	34
Llanfair fach and Bwlch gwynt	187	Fort Farm	28
Bwlch gwynt	6	Ffosglau	45
Llanfair House	8	Penlan goitre	9
Llwynpiod		Goitre fach	4
Weavers' Hall		Maesyfforest	18
Tivy View		Llwynfeilig and Ty canol	19
Wernfawr	66	Rhos feilig	7
Part of llywnieir	8	Pencaerodyn	34
Llanfair fach and Bwlch gwynt	187	Fort Farm	28
Bwlch gwynt	6	Ffosglau	45
Llanfair House	8	Penlan goitre	9
Llwynpiod		Goitre fach	4

Llanfair Clydogau Valuation Survey, 1910 - 1915				
Building/Land	Acres	Building/Land	Acres
Weavers' Hall		Maesfforest	18
Tivy View		Llwynfeilig and Ty canol	19
Wernfawr	66	Rhos feilig	7
Powell Hill	20	Nantybwch	2
Powell Hill Cottage		Penlanmedd	139
Islwyn House		Allotment	71
Glandulas	73	Cefnfoelallt	60
Fflosglau Cottage		Alltlynog	10
Pantynos	48	Pengraig	3
Brondeifi	3	Glanrafon	26
Llanfair Factory		Cwrtycylchau	12
Garreg ddu		Wauncastle	16
Temple Bar		Penbryn	3
Rallt	7	Ynysmoch	8
Tanybryn		Troedybryn	8
Rallt Cottage and old Plas	4	Cnwcsych	8
Sarn Llys and Mountain Gate	12	Ochrbryn	25
Pencilboa	10	Talwrnglas uchaf (land)	8
Pretoria		Penrhiw	11
Pant y Manol	2	Pantyfedwen	22
Llwyn Bedw	7	Maes glas	15
Lluastybedw	10	Tynywaun	9
Henlluastybedw	1	Blaenwaun (land)	22
Oxen hall	7	Pant Teg (land)	5

Llanfair Clydogau Valuation Survey, 1910 - 1915			
Building/Land	Acres	Building/Land	Acres
Frondeg	13	Brynglas and Cefnbryn	44
Wenallt Isaf	9	Brynmeiog	18
Lluast Isaf	10	Blaennant	16
Esgair	28	Ddeunant	17
Nantyclawdd	8	Meolfryn	21
Blaencwbugail (land)	3	Pantymeiniog	27
Brynmine	14	Esgairwen	25
Gwarffynon	23	Blaenplwyfr	15
Lluest uchaf	13	Ffosyffin	14
Llwyngog	1	Pengelli Bryn	24
Greenfield		Wenallt uchaf	2
Troedrhiwcoch	23	Pengelli esgair	37
Esgairmaen	51	Blaenyresgair	6
Cefnresgair	17	Blaencyswch allotment	22
Part of Blaencyswch allotment	3	Nantybwch Allotment	6
Pantyresgair	21	Glanyrafon Cottage	
Bulah	5	Esgerenglish	
Cwmyolchfa	5	Llanfairfach (woodland)	6
Tanresgair	9	Powell Hill (woodland)	2
Glanrhyd	11	Woodland around Maesyfforest and sporting rights of Derry Ormand	890
Glanrafon uchaf		Sporting rights of Llanfair estate of Glan Denys	2009

Llanfair Clydogau Valuation Survey, 1910 - 1915			
Building/land	**Acres**	**Building/land**	**Acres**
Blaennant (land)	1	Sporting rights near Blaen plwyfr of Falcondale	82
Castle Hill	62	Llanfair Mount (land)	6

The original document also shows the name of the land owner and tenant. The largest land owners were:

1. The Trustees of the late Carwyn Jones (Agent D. W. Drummond, Esq), Cawdor Estate Office, Carmarthenshire. They controlled the estate of the deceased William Jones of Glan Denys. The Trustrees owned, for instance: Llanfair Fawr, Pentre, Waunwen, Parcneuadd, Penlan, Nantymedd, Pentrelan, Clwrtypatrwm and Blaencwm;

2. Wilmot Inglis-Jones of Derry Ormond, who owned Blaenwern, Penlanmedd and a lot of property and land in the general area west of the Teifi.

In addition the record shows us that other notable local families with estates in other areas of Cardiganshire, owned land in Llanfair. For instance, Col. Davies Evans of Highmead, and G. C. Harford of Falcondale. We also see a recognition in the document of the holding of sporting rights across areas of the parish. Wilmot Inglis Jones, the Trustees of Mr. C. Jones and Mr. Harford are all shown as such.

If we were to compare this list of land and property with that shown in the 1839 tithe apportionment detail, we can see the extent to which the settlement of Llanfair had spread out from the Teifi valley up the highlands to

Chapter Six 1900 to 2008

Senior citizens near the smithy

the east and west, especially that land traversed by the River Clywedog's three tributaries. This is the area from which, as already reported, people began to retreat in the 19th century, and continued to do so, in large numbers later in this century as a growing realisation took place that the possibility of farming and living profitably on some of this land was impossible.

The Llanfair economy in 1910

Kelly's Directory[8] of 1910 gives a snapshot of the parish's economy. Letters were received at 10.30 am and dispatched at 1.20pm. The nearest money order office was Lampeter, and telegraph office was Llangybi. Wall letter boxes existed at Llanfair Factory and Penycraig. Commercial enterprises included: the Llanfair Bridge Inn; woollen manufacture at Weavers Hall and Llanfair Factory; carpenter at Glanrhyd and Tycoch;

shopkeeper at Llanfair Bridge and Cwrt y Cylchau; blacksmith at Llwyngog and a fulling mill at Pandy.

In addition to this published list there was also a blacksmith at Ty Gof, adjacent to the surviving buildings of the former lead and silver mine complex. In the early years of the century David Jones ran a smithy here. In the 1940's Beti Davies[9] used to visit her grandfather Benjamin Jones, who was then the proprietor. His account book of 1941 shows a new shovel being sold for 7s.6d and four horse shoes at 6s.6d. She told me that when she was eight or nine years of age she used to travel from her home at Cellan on a Saturday morning to assist her grandfather at the smithy. She helped by visiting hill and mountainside farms and smallholdings with a copy of their annual invoice from the smithy. She was told that if people could not pay cash that she should collect milk, butter or butter milk as an alternative form of payment.

The Poor Law.

The document, "An Assessment for the Relief of the Poor of Llanfair Clydogau[10] dated 19th November 1919, provides an insight into the working of a system which was the basis of assistance for those unfortunate enough to need public financial support. It is important to remember that this was a time when there was still no publicly available health care and no general or universal financial provision for anyone, except for a limited old age pension for the over 70's. The old and infirm, destitute, mentally ill, physically disabled and those with any other serious affliction which rendered them unable to work, or find work, had to depend upon their families to look after and support them. Those lacking such support could apply for a limited amount of public assistance. The funding for this system came from a levy which was applied to tenants of land and property. The 1915 detail for Llanfair Parish shows 256 separate units of property or land, listed by name, location and the person required to pay the financial levy specified. The number of recorded units considerably exceeded the number of actual houses shown within the 1901 census. A sample of payments required of the inhabitants of various properties, was as follows:

- Llanfair Fawr £9.6s.4d;
- Pentre £10.11s.9d;
- Wainwen £8.15s.0d;
- Parcneuadd £6.2s.11d;
- Nant y Medd £10.6s.6d;
- Penlan £6.0s.9d;
- Llanfair Fach £6.9s.6d;
- Blaen cwm £5.6s.9d;
- Llanfair Factory £2.2s.0d;
- Great Western Railway Company £0.14s.0d;
- Llanfair Chapel (land at Temple Bar) £0.4s.4d;
- Wilmot Inglis Jones, sporting rights over his Llanfair estates £1.8s.0d.

First World War (1914-18)

It is not known how many people from the parish were enrolled in the armed forces. Those who "joined up" or were conscripted would be drawn from an adult male population of about 160-170 people. The evidence suggests that men from Llanfair joined the forces in similar numbers to those of other communities throughout the British Isles.

There is no centrally available list for the parish of fatalities. Unusually no War Memorial was constructed in Llanfair, though there are commemorative plaques to some individual men in both St Mary's Church and Capel Mair. Two of the five men associated with the parish who are known to have died, are buried in the Churchyard and have military headstones of the type seen in graveyards to the British forces throughout the world.

Chapter Six   1900 to 2008

Lampeter "boys" under orders for the front

The details of those who are known to have died are as follows:

- Private David Lewis Davies of Weavers Hall,
  5th Battalion Kings Shropshire Light Infantry,
  Died 29th August 1916 in France.
  Plaque in remembrance in St Mary's Church.
  Commemorated on Thiepval Memorial to missing of the Somme;

- Private David Davies,
  Welsh Guards,
  Died 11th February 1917.
  Grave in Llanfair Churchyard;

- Private David Lloyd of Troedrhiwgoch,
  9th Battalion Welsh Regiment,
  Died 29th May 1917.
  Plaque in remembrance in Capel Mair.
  Grave in Klein-Vierstraat British Cemetery, Kemmel, Belgium;

- Private Evan David Williams (of 6 Greenfield Terrace, Lampeter)
  13th Battalion Welsh Regiment,
  Gassed in France, health broke down,
  Died at Ynys, Llanfair on 22nd July 1919, aged 20 years,
  Grave in Llanfair Churchyard.

- William Davies of Cefn Foelallt Uchaf,
  Welsh Regiment,
  Died in hospital in France on 5th November 1918, aged 30 years.

A commemorative statement to Pte. William Davies of Cefn Foelallt Uchaf, issued by his parents. (He was an uncle of Llanfair's current County Councillor, Odwyn Davies.)

First Wold War Roll of Honour

Until about 12 years ago St Mary's Church had a framed roll of honour hanging on the wall, listing church members who served in the First World War. Sadly it has disappeared. Thankfully a copy of a photograph of the roll with its names of parishioners has survived. The list below has been constructed using this faded photograph.

ROLL OF HONOUR

MEMBERS OF THIS CHURCH

SERVED IN THE EUROPEAN WAR

1914-1918

James Williams Pengraig
David Lewis Davies Weaver's Hall
John Davies Weaver's Hall
Tommie Williams Gwarffynnon
Timothy Rees Davies Bronteify
Charlie A. Edwards Rhiw
David Jones Glancrwys
David John Williams Llwyngog
Evan Rees Williams Llwyngog
Benjamin T. Jones Office Fach
John Roderick Evans Office Fawr
John Evan Jones Silvermine
David Williams Esgair mine
John David Edward Evans Llanfair Fawr
Richard Hughes Bronfa
Hughie Hughes Bronfa
Tommie Hughes Bronfa
Stephen Jenkins Maes Glas
Dan Jones Pantffin
Evan David Williams Ynys
William Davies Cefn Foelallt
Willie Rees Davies Blaen Cyswcch

(Compiled in August 2008, from a photograph of a very faded, water damaged original, which is missing from St Mary's Church)

Chapter Six   1900 to 2008

In an effort to support the Red Cross during the War, the Lampeter Agricultural Society held a large jumble sale in December 1915 covering many local parishes. The sale raised £287.5s.6d, of which the residents of Llanfair contributed £40.8s.5d. Efforts were made to enlist the parish population into saving to fund the cost of the war, and various officials visited Llanfair School to talk to the children about the importance of the savings movement.

July 18th 1919 was declared "Peace Day" in the school and the children were given the afternoon off. The following day many people in the parish held a celebratory tea and sports event to recognise "Peace Day".

Peace Day celebration at Llanfair, 1919

Parish tragedies in the early 19th century

The following details have been extracted from the burial records of the church:

- David Williams of Glandulas Isaf, Llangybi, aged 17, buried 25th July 1905, "drowned in the Teifi";
- Richard Williams of Beulah, aged 50, buried by Coroners Order, "drowned in the Tivy";
- Thomas Anthony Davies of Llanddewi Brefi, aged 25, buried 16th May 1911, "killed by lightning";
- John Lloyd Williams of Gwarffynon, aged 41, buried 9th July 1914, "killed by a horse at LLechryd- Coroner's Order";
- Jenkin Williams of Pentre, aged 4, buried 10th November 1924, "death by drowning- Coroner's Order";
- David Aeron Jones of Llanddewi Brefi, aged 18, buried 4th June 1937, "Coroner's Order, gun accident".

Llanfair Agricultural Show.

The Llanfair Show was an important event in the life of the parish. At its creation it was to be an annual event, the first of these being held on 27th August 1919. As an idea it perhaps arose out of the spirit of optimism which accompanied a return to civil normality after the end of the First World War, prior to the drop of 23% in the parish population between 1921 and 1931. There was already in existence, the longer established and better known Lampeter Agricultural Society. The Lampeter Show, which had been founded earlier, was re formed in 1887, when a committee was set up with its first patron being William Jones of Glandenys, who was by then, the major land owner of Llanfair. He was joined by several other members of the local gentry. There were clearly important links between the Lampeter organisation and Llanfair parish in as much as in 1920 Mr J. Evans of Llanfair Fawr, and in 1926 Mr. B.L.Jones of Llanfair Bridge and Mr J Lloyd-Jones of Llanfair Fach, were committee members of the Lampeter Show.

The recollection of people in the parish today, is that the Llanfair Show ran successfully until 1929 or perhaps 1930 which is believed to be the last. The Show was organised by a committee. The photograph below shows committee members posing for a photograph outside Llanfair Fawr, along with the President, Mrs Anne Jones of Glandenys.

Llanfair Show members 1925

Glyn Evans of Gogoyan, later Esgairmaen.

The public poster advertising the Show in 1919 is an excellent example of the social inter relationship of members of the land owning group with members of the local farming community. An extract from this poster is shown below.

The 25 Vice Presidents included Mrs Inglis Jones of Derry Ormond, Lt. Co. Delme Davies-Evans, DSO of Golden Grove, E. H. Formby Esq., Ald. R. S. Rowland, The Garth, Dr. Evan Evans, Lampeter; D Lloyd-Lewis, Esq., Ivy Bush and D. I. Rees, Esq., Auctioneer, Velindre. The actual organisation of the Show lay in the hands of Llanfair residents, especially its Secretary Mr. T. M Griffiths of Blaencwm and its Treasurer Jonathan Williams of Pentre. There were competitions for horses, including one with a prize given by Edward Formby (the friend of Mrs Anne Jones of Glandenys, see below, the section on the graves), available only for tenants of the Glandenys Estate. Other competitions included: cattle; farm produce; fruit and vegetables; horticultural; butter; cheese and both foot races and trotting races.

Llanfair Show 1925 in Llanfair Fawr field

The photograph above shows the 1925 Show on land opposite the church, with some early automobiles in view.

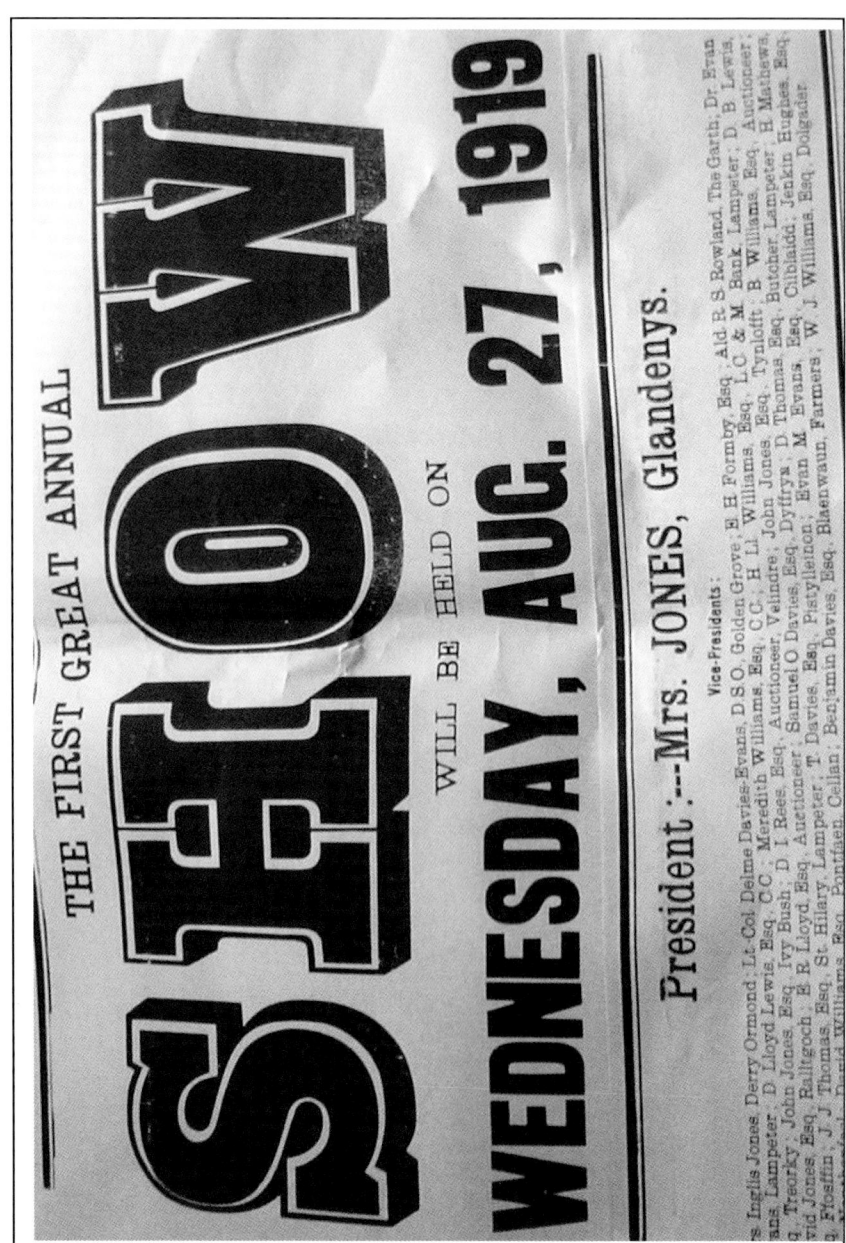

Third Annual Show : 1921

President : Mrs. Anne Jones, Glandenys

General Manager : Mr. E. H. Formby

Vice Manager : Mr. D.W. Griffiths, Blaencwm

Chairman : John Williams, Penlanmedd

Vice Chairman : John Herbert, Llanfair Fach

Treasurer : Mr. H. Lloyd-Williams and
Jonathan Williams, Pentre

Secretary : Mr. T. M. Griffiths, Blaencwm

Stewards :

- Mr. T. Davies, Post Office;
- John Lloyd Jones, Graigddu-uchaf;
- Ben Jones, Office Fach;
- Joseph Evans, Llanfair Fawr;
- Reuben Pates, Gelly;
- Timothy Davies, Cefnfoelallt;
- Daniel Evans, Glanrhyd;
- D. Richards, Silvermine;
- Joseph Rees, Cefnfoelallt;
- Evans Evan, Esgairmaen.

Chapter Six　　　　　　　　　　　　　　　　　　　　1900 to 2008

The Show President of the inaugural event, Anne Jones died in March 1929 at the age of 78. The Catalogue for the 11th annual "Show and Races" of that summer illustrates the extent to which the structure of society was changing. The historically significant local gentry of the First Show had largely disappeared. Instead the President was local farmer, Joseph Evans, J.P. of Llanfair Fawr and there was by now no attempt to list a range of local dignitaries as Vice Presidents, merely the members of the organising committee. They were H. Lewis of Waunwen, E. R. Jones of Llanfair Mill, D. James of Penddol and J. T. Jones of Llwynieir, Lampeter. The range of competitive classes was not dissimilar to that of the inaugural show. One new class was for the "best pair of plain hand knitted gent's stockings, with a first prize of £1". This class was "in remembrance of the late President, Mrs Jones of Glandenys".

The Llanfair Show had a range of cups for the different competitive classes. These were given by members of the local landowning or business community. As an indication, the cup "for the best group of sheep" was the Challenge Cup, presented in 1926 by H.J. Williams, Esq. of the Llanfair Bridge Hotel in 1926. Some of these cups are understood to have been incorporated into the Lampeter Show following the demise of the Llanfair event.

The ending of the Llanfair Show saw local farmers continuing their involvement with farm shows principally through the auspices of the Lampeter Show. The minutes[11] of the Lampeter Agricultural Society record Mr. J. Evans of Llanfair Fawr and Mr. J. Lloyd-Jones of Llanfair Fach being appointed by the committee to canvass for new members in the Llanfair and Llanddewi areas at about this time. This Show was very long established and extremely important within the wider area. Interestingly in 1861, the award for the best farm in the show went to David Thomas of Llanfair Fach and the judge, Joseph Jenkins of Swansea wrote a poem about this, as follows:

PRICE SIXPENCE.

LLANFAIR-CLYDOGAU

AGRICULTURAL AND HORTICULTURAL SOCIETY.

THE ELEVENTH ANNUAL

SHOW & RACES

WILL BE HELD ON

Wednesday, Sept. 4th., 1929

On a field kindly lent by the President.

President: JOSEPH EVANS, Esq., J.P., Llanfairfawr.
General Manager: D. W. GRIFFITHS, Esq., Pentre.

CATALOGUE OF ENTRIES.

TEA WILL BE PROVIDED.

Admission to the Show Field 1s. 3d. ; Children 8d.

Chairman—H. LEWIS, Esq., Waunwen.
Vice-Chairman—E. R. JONES, Esq., Llanfair Mill.
Hon Treasurer—D. JAMES, Esq., Penddol.
Hon. Secretary.—J. T. JONES, Llwynieir, Lampeter.

D. R. Evans & Co., The Bridge Press, Lampeter.

"As David Thomas, Llanfair
Is such a tenant farmer
Let him have a durable lease
If that will please his master"[12].

The Llanfair Show was still a subject of discussion many years later. For instance, at a meeting of the Llanfair Parish Council in 1974, the minutes state,

" The Clerk was asked to publicise that a Parish Council meeting for all the electors of Llanfair Clydogau be held at the Church Hall on Friday 5th April at 8.00 pm, to discuss the money invested at the Midland Bank from the Llanfair Agricultural Show[13].

Subsequent minutes do not show either the amount of money involved or what decision was taken concerning this money. However, Ian Evans[14] of Esgair Maen told me he believed the meeting decided to disperse the money on the basis of £90 each to St Mary's and Capel Mair, and to give the main cup of the Show to the Lampeter Show, for incorporation into that event.

The Graves near "the hill of the holy place"

These graves known locally as "the lovers' graves", are located on the edge of "the hill of the holy place" (Bryn Cysegrfan), and are those of Mrs Anne Jones and Mr. Edward Hesketh Formby, both of Glandenys, Betws Bledrws. The two individuals featured prominently in the first Llanfair Show of 1919. Mrs Jones was the President and Mr Formby, a Vice President. Though the publicity for the Show lists his name, his residence is carefully not shown, presumably because of the delicate public position of his relationship with the widowed Anne Jones. This relationship is explored by Bethan Phillips in her book, "The Lovers' Graves[15]. The graves are located to the rear of the ruined building of Tan y Bryn, close to Plas yr Allt at the point where the Teifi valley side begins to slope steeply upwards to Bryn Cysegrfan. The funerals of the two individuals were major events in the life of the parish in the 1920's and both took place at St Mary's Church.

Graves of Anne Jones and Edward Hesketh Formby at Tan y Bryn

Funeral cortege of Edward Hesketh Formby leaving Llanfair Church for private burial

Attention within the parish and the wider area had been focused upon the Jones family of Glandenys for some time because of the wealth and importance of William Jones, the banker of Glandenys. In 1868 this attention was increased when he bought some of the Llanfair estate of Lord

Chapter Six   1900 to 2008

Carrington. Before that he featured in the history of Llanfair, in that his banking company was involved in taking out a writ against the Rev. Morgan Williams for his unpaid loan. Also, in 1860 we saw his support for the appointment of the Rev. William Evans of Silian, to the vacant position of Perpetual Curate of Llanfair and Llangybi. As a result of his purchase of the estate he became the person to whom a large number of tenant farmers paid their rents. He also became one of the two landowners alternatively responsible for the appointment of a minister to the position of Perpetual Curate whenever a vacancy occurred. In 1877 at the age 65, William Jones married his wife Anne, aged 23. They lived together at Glandenys. In the 1890's, Edward Formby, a younger man than Anne, became her friend and companion and joined her and her husband at the Glandenys house.

William Jones died in January 1897 at the age of 85. His funeral took place at Llanfair Church on 12th January. This recognised his position as the premier landowner in the parish and his senior role as a patron of the church. The funeral service was conducted by three clergymen, the Dean of Gloucester (married to William Jones's niece Mary Eleanor Geraldine Jones), the Vicar of Lampeter and J.N. Evans, Vicar of Llanfair. He was buried in the graveyard. His wife continued to live with Edward Formby at Glandenys, but unusually did not inherit the estate of her husband.

His will[16] was constructed a year into his marriage and before the arrival on the scene of Edward Formby. In this document of 31st December 1878, William Jones had appointed his brother John Jones and his nephew Frederick Arthur Gerwyn Jones, as "Trustees and Executors and after certain bequests and other dispositions, devised his Manor of Cellan and all other manors, lands, tenements and real estate unto the said John Jones and Gerwyn Jones and their heirs".

When Edward Formby died in 1926 at the age of 60, though his funeral took place at Llanfair Church, his request was to be buried in an unmarked grave on the lower slopes of Bryn Cysegrfan at a spot where he had bought land. He bought this from Mrs Thomas of Gwarffordd and Tom Thomas[17] has explained how his mother was paid 5/- per annum for keeping the grave(s) neat and tidy. The burial entry for Mr. Formby shows his funeral ceremony in the church being performed by J. N. Evans, Vicar and J H. Davies, Vicar of Silian. Photographs of the time suggest it was a large and impressive funeral with burial at his chosen place.

In 1929 Anne Jones died at the age of 78. Her funeral service also took place in Llanfair Church prior to burial, according to the church register, "in an enclosed plot near Plas, Llanfair Clydogau Parish". This was the private location of the earlier burial of her companion. Once again the photographs of the time show a very large well attended funeral, including a considerable presence at the graveside. Johnny Williams,[18] formerly of Cellan told me of his recollection as a seven year old who accompanied his father to Llanfair on this day. He said that there was a very large number of people lined up outside the walled churchyard to watch the horse drawn cart move slowly away towards the unusual and remote burial location. The body had been carried on an open wagon pulled by horses all the way from the family home at Glandenys near Silian. Bleddyn Williams,[19] relative of a farmer near the mansion, told me that the coffin was covered in moss prior to its journey and that the cart and horses came from the nearby Coed Parc.

The two graves of Edward Hesketh Formby and Anne Jones lie side by side on sloping land surrounded by trees immediately to the rear of the ruined and now abandoned, Tan y bryn. It is a quiet and very peaceful spot. There are no gravestones but the two mounds which mark the graves can be clearly seen.

Tom Thomas explained how the road leading to the graves and his home became known as Formby's Lane.

1920's the Glebe land.

By the 1920's Llanfair and Llangybi each had their own Anglican ministers. In 1920 the Rev. J.N. Evans[20] described the Glebe lands of the Llanfair parish as comprising 258 acres spread over four parishes. These included lands in Llanwrda and Pencarreg and he received the rents of £145 as a major part of his income. At the same time the vicar of Llangybi received rents of £103 per annum from his four properties on that parish's Glebe land.

Where Glebe lands still exist today, they are administered by the Church Commissioners in Wales and not individual parishes, and rents which are received, help to fund the overall operation of the church within the Principality.

The Women's Institute

The Llanfair Clydogau Women's Institute (W.I.), is a significant social grouping within the parish. It was established in 1926 jointly with Cellan parish, based upon a model of that which emerged across England and Wales following the creation of the first WI in 1915 in Anglesey.

Llanfair and Cellan Women's Institute, circa 1947 outside Llanfair Church Hall

In the 1950's, Llanfair split from Cellan and became exclusively Llanfair W.I. It is open to any woman in the area for an annual subscription.

Chapter Six — 1900 to 2008

Membership of the Llanfair WI in 1970 totalled 21, it had declined to 10 in 1986, but has risen steadily in recent years, now standing at an impressive 27 in 2008. This constitutes a combination of Welsh speakers, some of whom have lived in Llanfair for all, or most of their life, and English "incomers". It makes for a very harmonious mix and those attending speak highly of the quality of the local organisation.

Meetings take place monthly throughout the year in the Church Hall, which more recently has become known as the Village Hall, with guest speakers. On occasions when it is thought that the theme of the speaker may be of local interest, they are declared "open meetings" and members of other WI's and the local community in general are invited. Funds are raised principally from the portion of the annual subscription which is able to be retained, rather than be sent to headquarters and from regular fundraising activities held each year, such as the Cawl and Whist held in March and the Twmpath Dawns ("Barn Dance"), held usually in November or December. Photographs within this publication show a number of its functions, in particular the celebrations of the 21st, 50th and 60th years of its foundation.

Celebration of 21 years

Celebration of 50 years

Celebration of 60 years

Sale of the Glandenys Estate[21] in 1930

Symptomatic of the major changes taking place within the area, was the continuing breakup of the large land holdings owned by a few individuals.

1868 had seen the sale of some of Lord Carrington's Llanfair estate to William Jones of Glandenys. Following his death in 1897, and then the death of his wife Anne in 1929, the Glandenys Estate was put up for sale, with some properties being sold prior to the auction of 2nd May 1930. There were 78 to be disposed of in all. These were located in Llanfair Clydogau, Cellan, Llanddewi Brefi, Llanfihangel Ystrad, Lampeter and Silian parishes. The Llanfair properties sold were:

- Llanfair Fawr, (247.819 acres);
- Office Fach;,
- Maesyfforest (4.681 acres);
- Llanfair Bridge Inn;
- Silvermine Cottages, Nos 1, 2, 3 and 4;
- Rhiw;
- Caeglas and Llanfair Mill, (53.300 acres);
- Caeglas Allotment;
- Esgerddu, (31.944 acres);
- Hendrebant, (9.669 acres);
- Llanfair Shop;
- Pandy House and Land, (5.256 acres);
- Gellydyfod, (42.809 acres);
- Gelly Allotment, (26.499 acres);
- Pentrelan, (78.803 acres);
- Blaencwm, (74.643 acres);
- Waunwen, (234.796 acres);
- Clwt-Patrwn, (76.501 acres);
- Clwt-Patrwn Allotment (45 acres)

Chapter Six   1900 to 2008

- Parcneuadd, (92.805 acres);
- Nantymedd,(172.797 acres);
- Nantymedd Allotment, (172.971 acres);
- Tycoch, (7.773 acres);
- Land, formerly part of Parcneuadd, (24.147 acres);
- Land, formerly part of Parcneuadd, (7 acres);
- Llanfair Meadows, (23.648 acres) (near Nantymedd);
- Pentre, (190.123 acres);
- Pentre Allotment, (153.367 acres);
- Office Fawr Cottage, (4.086 acres);
- Penlan, (193.703 acres);
- Gwarffordd and Gwarallt, (14.400 acres);
- Wenallt Issa, (22.667 acres);
- Bryn Allotment, (5.987 acres) (near Pengelli'r bryn);
- Esgermine, (6.464 acres);
- Penygarn Allotment, (5.228 acres) (near Esgermine).

Sale of the Derry Ormond Estate [22] in 1944

As the century progressed, the decline in the number of large estates and the break up of the historic pattern of land holdings continued, with further societal changes. Many tenant farmers moved to purchase the land they farmed and the farm buildings where they had lived, in some cases for generations. The last of the large local sales occurred in 1944 with the auction to dispose of the major portion of the Derry Ormond estate which had been owned by the Inglis-Jones family. The major sale consisting of lots either in Llanfair or on the edge of the parish, was as follows:

- Goitre Issa, (114 acres);
- Goitre Fach, (4 acres);
- Nantybwch, (59 acres);

- Penlangoitre, (10 acres);
- Llwynfeilig, (60 acres);
- Blaenwern, (120 acres);
- Ffosglai Wood, (36 acres);
- Long Wood ,(105 acres);
- Allt Cefn foel, (19 acres);
- Pantglas Plantation, (25 acres);
- Glandulais Ucha, (108 acres).

Second World War (1939-45)

No figures are available with regard to recruitment into the armed forces from the parish of Llanfair. It would have taken place from an adult population of about 210, of whom about 100 would be male. However, we have some knowledge about numbers involved from various sources. Those from the St Mary's Church records, show which of its parishioners were "on Active Service or war work as of 1944."

(Source church Vestry records)

Name	House	Service
Jenkin Aneurin Jones	Llanfair Shop	RAF
Thomas Thomas	Gwarffordd	RAF
Eiluned Davies	Cnwcsych	WAAF
Allenby Powell	Beulah	R. Navy
Morgan Gwyn Stephens	Gwarffynnon	War work
Benjamin Stephens	Gwarffynnon	RAF
Thomas Williams	Llwyngog	War work
Ivor Williams	Llwyngog	Army

We know that at least three men from the parish died in the War. The detail is as follows:

- Sergeant Benjamin Lloyd-Jones of Troedybryn,
  220 Squadron, Royal Air Force.
  Died 5th August 1941, aged 22.
  Commemorated on Runnymede Memorial.
  Plaque of remembrance within St Mary's Church;

- Driver Evan Lloyd-Jones of Troedybryn,
  Royal Army Service Corps.
  Died 20th April 1942, aged 27.
  Plaque of remembrance within St Mary's Church.
  Grave in Llanfair Clydogau churchyard;

Grave headstone in Llanfair graveyard to:

Evan Lloyd-Jones and his brother, Benjamin, both of Troedybryn.

- Private Evan Thomas of Llwyn,
  Australian Imperial Forces.
  Died 21st March 1945, aged 38 after capture in Singapore.
  Plaque of remembrance within St Mary's Church.
  Grave in Borneo.

Llanfair Clydogau Welcome Home Fund

A decision was taken to create a fund for those parishioners who had "served their King and Country in her hour of need and will share the Welcome Home Fund". The detail of the organising committee is interesting in that it shows, amongst the relatively small population of this community, the key role occupied by farmers Gwyn Evans of Llanfair Fawr, (Chairman and Collector), Mr. J.T. Jones of Waunwen, (Secretary and Collector), Mr. W. Lloyd-Jones of Llanfair Fach, (Treasurer) and Miss Eiddwen James, (Organiser of Concerts, Sports, etc) headteacher of the school. The same people are reported upon in regard to other parish activities elsewhere within this book. The Committee collected £425.1s.10d, with most households making a donation.

The list of those parishioners who received donations from the Fund is shown below. The amounts allocated were graded, hence it is assumed that someone undertook an assessment as to how long the service person was away, or degree of conflict and potential danger faced. Of the three men from the parish who died in the war, the family of Evan and Benjamin Lloyd Jones received the largest amount, being given £15.15s for each son. The family of the third soldier, Evan Thomas, was only allocated £2. Presumably this was because at the end of the 1930's he had left Llwyn to emigrate to Australia and it was in fighting as a member of the Australian forces in Singapore that he was captured by Japanese forces.

Chapter Six   1900 to 2008

The document describing the allocations to those who served stated:

"These will receive £15.15s each:

- Mr E. Lloyd Jones of Troedybryn
- Mr B. Lloyd Jones of Troedybryn
- Mr Gethin Jones, Llanfair Post Office
- Mr D. Jenkins Jones, Llanfair Fach
- Mr J. Llewelyn Jones, Llanfair Fach
- Mr Dyfrig Powell, Beulah
- Mr Allenby Powell, Beulah
- Mr Emlyn Powell, Troedybryn
- Mr Edward Davies, Pantyfedwen
- Mr Oswald Davies, Glanrafon
- Mr James Davies, Glanrafon
- Mr Raymond Griffiths, Goitre Fach
- Mr Walter Griffiths, Goitre Fach
- Mr Mansel Evans, Fort Farm
- Mr J.D. Evans, Noyadd
- Mr Tommy Davies, Tancoed
- Mr Ivor Williams, Llwyngog
- Mr Tommy Thomas, Gwarffordd
- Mr Benjamin Stephens, Gwarffynon

These will receive £11.5s each:

- Mr Aneurin Jones, Llanfair Post Office
- Mr David Davies, Llaingoch
- Mr Tommy Rees, Iscoed

These will receive £8.5s each:

- Mr David Jenkins, late Maesglas
- Mr Eurwin Jenkins, late Maesglas
- Mr T.H. Williams, late Penlanmedd
- Mr Dan Jones, late Smithy
- Mr Dan Ebernezer, late Pantresger
- Mrs Doreen Pickstone, Pantresger
- Miss Mary Davies, Parkypowell

These will receive the sum of £2 each as an appreciation of their services, as passed at the Public Meeting held on January 10th 1946:

- Evan Thomas, late of Llwyn
- Mr Sidney Jenkins, Lluest
- Mrs Eluned Williams, late of Cnwcsych
- Mr Osmond Jones, late of Pantymanal
- Mr Tim Rees, late of Efailfach
- Mr Evan Rees, late of Efailfach
- Mr Ian James, late of Glanrafon
- Mr John James, late of Glanrafon
- Mr William Rayments, late of Rhiw
- Mr James Jones, Fachddu
- Mr Tommy Jones, late of Brynmenog
- Miss Aeronwy Jones, late of Brynmenog
- Mrs Ceridwen Brooksbanks, late of Llanfair Mill
- Mr S.D. Jones, late of Llanfair Mill."

There are 43 people named within the resolution reproduced above. That is a large number, drawn from a parish population of about 210 adults.

Chapter Six   1900 to 2008

Parish Memorial Fund for Second World War dead

On 14th March 1955 a meeting was convened at the primary school to decide how to create a memorial to the "three fallen heroes from the parish". It was convened by Sylvan Griffiths and Eiddwen James. A decision was taken to make a collection across the parish in order to fund a lectern and litany desk in the parish church. A total of £126.6s.0d was donated in the form of 92 family, or individual amounts. The planned lectern and litany desk, together with an attached inscription naming the three dead servicemen, was subsequently purchased.

The minutes of the church's Easter Vestry meeting for 1956 record as follows, "Memorial Lectern and Litany Desk. Reference was made to the parish collection made in order to install a Lectern and Litany Desk at St Mary's Church as a memorial to three local men who had made the supreme sacrifice in World War II". An application to the Diocesan Faculty Board for permission to install this was granted later. At a subsequent meeting it was reported that Messrs. Mailes were executing the furnishings and that the Lord Bishop would officiate for the dedication on 24th October 1956.

This Memorial Lectern, together with Commemorative Plaque, is the one which stands at the front of the church today, with which those who attend the annual parish Christmas Carol Concert will be familiar.

Cardiganshire Home Guard

On 14th May 1940, Sir Anthony Eden, Secretary of State for War, appealed in a broadcast for volunteers to join a Defence Force designed to protect the country from invasion. Brigadier Taylor-Lloyd[23] has written that following the request for volunteers, he attended a meeting called by the Lord Lieutenant (the Earl of Lisburne), at Crosswood, to discuss the next steps. He reports that the Lord Lieutenant said that His Majesty the King had called upon all Lord Lieutenants to raise a Defence Force for the protection of the country. The Earl stated that he would take command of this force in Cardiganshire, with Brigadier Taylor-Lloyd as second in command. However, the Lord Lieutenant was quickly called upon to rejoin the Welsh Guards and as a result, Brigadier Taylor-Lloyd became commander. By September 1940 over 3,000 men had enrolled across the county. The force was initially called "The Local Defence Volunteers" before a name change to Home Guard.

The Llanfair part of Cardiganshire was covered by the work of the 3rd Battalion. The three Cardiganshire battalions operated until 3rd December 1944 when "stand down" was announced. Their role had been to be prepared to defend this area against a possible invasion. They were part of a network of similar units across the United Kingdom. By August 1944 there were 1,727,000 men enrolled in the Home Guard, and women Home Guard Auxiliaries, (of whom there were some in Cardiganshire), totalled 30,696.

A number of men from Llanfair were in the Home Guard. Those shown in the photograph of the No 2 Platoon, Llanddewi Brefi below, are Mr. G. Evans of Llanfair Fawr, Mr. R. Pates of Gelli Ddyfod, Mr. D. J. Morgan of Ty Coch and Mr. J. Lloyd of Pantynos.

Chapter Six   1900 to 2008

W.R. Lloyd Jones (Llanfair Fach) of the Home Guard

In Cardiganshire as a whole, the Home Guard had to perform a wide variety of tasks ranging from observing, to being ready to engage in armed conflict in the event of an enemy invasion. One of the most unusual activities related to the work of the Home Guard unit established in the Tregaron area, was the task of patrolling the very remote mountainous area to the east of the town. The photograph below shows this specialist group near to Ffrwd ar Gamddwr at a height of about 1500 feet. Third from the left is David Jones of Nantymaen, the father of Deborah Jones of Llanfair Fach. The other men in the group all lived in the small number of very isolated farms on either side of the Tregaron to Abergwesyn Road, such as Nantymaen, Maesglas and Nant llwyd.

Evacuees from the cities

During the War a number of children were moved from some of the most heavily bombed areas of England to the safer surroundings of Llanfair. It is believed that the number could have been as many as 20 youngsters. They lived with local families and attended Llanfair School. Their family homes were in Liverpool, Birmingham and London.

Home Guard members on patrol, east of Tregaron.

The 1941-3 Government Farm Survey[24]

The Government's intention was to gather information about all farms in England and Wales of over five acres. Data was collected on crops, livestock, labour, machinery and the "quality" of the farmer. The survey was dated 1943 for this parish and reported that 54 farming units exceeded five acres. It revealed much significant information about both the nature of the farming being carried out and the social conditions. For instance, 46 farms had at least one milk cow (12 had a single animal for milk purposes), and the largest number of cows being milked was 18 both at Llanfair Fawr and Llanfair Fach. Most places undertaking dairy farming also had other cows or calves and 33 farms had sheep. The largest numbers were 336 at Pentre, 292 at Penlan Medd, 272 at Nant y Medd and 236 at Waunwen. There was at least one pig at 30 separate farms, with some 20 of this total possessing only one animal. There were reports from 45 properties that they owned poultry with 31 residences owning one or more horses. These were the major means of providing power for ploughing and the hauling of carts or farm appliances. Many farms reported that they grew potatoes, oats and hay.

Washing the sheep at Cwm y Olchfa, a timeless activity, this photograph is post war

Fully operational water wheels were recorded at 11 farms including Llanfair Fawr, Pentre, Waunwen, Llanfair Mill, Blaencwm, Penlan,

Chapter Six　　　　　　　　　　　　　　　　1900 to 2008

Nant y Medd, Pandy, Llanfair Fach and Penlan Medd. Tractors had begun to appear relatively recently and the survey records these vehicles at Penlan, Llanfair Fach and Penlan Medd. The data also shows that there was no mains electricity or water supply at any farm, though several of the larger farms reported that they had piped water from their own sources. Water was obtained from private springs and wells.

Shearing party at Llanfair Fawr, a timeless activity, this photograph is of 1957

The electricity situation was fairly similar throughout Wales. The high capital cost of running cables into country areas meant that the rural areas were largely ignored until well after the War. A complete analysis of the National Farm Survey reveals that in 1941, only 8% of Welsh farms had a public electricity supply. In Cardiganshire the figure was even lower at 2%. It took until 1965 for 94% of Welsh farms to receive mains electricity[25].

The 1941 survey also contained a question on "Management". It asked the question, is your farm classified as A, B or C? (A highest and C the lowest grade). For those who had classified their farm as B or C it asked the farmer to tick a box giving a reason for their choice. The allowable reasons identified by the Government were: "old age", "lack of capital" or "personal failings". For those who selected personal failings as the reason for the low grade they had ascribed to themselves, the questionnaire then went on to ask for detail as to what these failings might be. In a number of cases where "personal failings" had been listed for Llanfair properties, the respondent in providing supplementary detail wrote as their reason for these failings, "lack of ambition".

In analysing the Llanfair data, the broad picture is of the enormous disparity in farming between the bigger farms with large amounts of lower land or valley bottom pastures, and the smaller units on the edges of the uplands. In the case of the latter, farming was very much how it would have been a hundred years before. These farms were on the least attractive and most marginal land, and the farmers tried to shape an economic livelihood which was almost a self sufficiency subsistence activity, with a dairy cow for milk, a pig for meat, chickens for eggs and meat, a horse for ploughing, crops planted for the production of potatoes for family food, and oats and hay for animal food, with a few sheep or calves for sale. Some of these small units did try to supplement their income by producing goods for sale. For instance Evan Davies[26] can recall in 1950, his family's larger farm of Pentrelan assisting smallholder neighbours along Sarn Helen to carry their milk down to the milk stand in the Teifi Valley bottom using a horse and cart. The milk in churns would then be taken by lorry to the local dairy at Llanio (on the Manchester and Milford Railway to the north).

Tom Thomas'[27] recollections of life in the 1930's very much confirms the pattern detailed in the Farm Survey. His mother farmed with about four cows and a number of sheep and chickens. She sold butter and eggs to a shopkeeper who called and tooted his horn at the bottom of Formby's Lane to let her know he had arrived. "She said that as long as the price of the butter paid to her did not fall below 1/- (5p) a pound, and the eggs 9d (4p) a dozen, she could make ends meet.". She also sold cheese and had regular customers. He explained how pig killing in the area was staggered. For instance, Waunwen, Penddol, Pantynos and his home at Gwarffordd, carried out the annual killing of a farm pig in stages, and then shared the faggots between them so that they could all have a succulent supply for several weeks. There was never any financial transaction. He also explained how big farms would often let the smaller farmers who did not have enough land upon which to grow potatoes, plant a few rows in their fields on condition that they gave assistance with the potato picking.

It is not surprising that the number of the smallest units steadily declined as the century progressed. Some became amalgamated into larger holdings with the farm house abandoned, others sold the land to the Forestry Commission for the planting of the large forestry plantations. These are much in evidence on the higher reaches of the Clywedog valley and at Longwood on the ridge between Llanfair and Llangybi today. A number of the upland farm buildings have survived, sometimes after a period of being empty, and are today occupied mainly by English people who have either moved to the area, or are using them as holiday homes.

Derelict Llanfair farms

A number of farm buildings which have become derelict during the 20th century are shown below. In 1954 the Welsh Agricultural Land Sub Commission[28], under the Welsh Department of the Ministry of Agriculture, Fisheries and Food, began a special investigation into the agricultural economy existing along a transect of the uplands of central Wales. The reference area included most of eastern Cardiganshire, along with areas which are now part of Powys. Of the 1,404 farms within the area which were examined in detail, the Report concluded that 57% were too small to be considered efficient economic units, whilst another 31% of them were only marginal, leaving only 12% that could be considered as profitable enterprises. Many had no tractors or any form of mechanised transport and

Nant y Clawd

Wenallt Uchaf

Wenallt Isaf

Cwm y Olchfa

1200 had no electricity, whilst 70% had no piped supply of water into the house in spite of rainfall averages of 50-100 inches. The Report also indicated that there was already a steady movement of people away from the most uneconomic farm units and a growth in larger farms as the more successful farmers took over the land of neighbours. This change in the population distribution can be seen in Llanfair with the abandonment of smallholdings, the movement of population away and the increase in size of some of the larger farm units.

An alternative lifestyle: inward migration.

The Rev. Williams in his excellent and informative book of 1966, foresaw only further gloom for the eastern uplands. He expected the enormous depopulation which he wrote about to continue after this date. He would have been surprised to have seen only a partial realisation of his forecast because, since the 1970's, at the same time as local residents were continuing to move away in search of a more secure economic future in areas where greater opportunities existed in South Wales, London or elsewhere in Britain, a small but significant inward movement of people began to occur. The incomers were largely English, seeking a slower more reflective and peaceful way of life, perhaps more space, more opportunities for individualism or a greater possibility of self expression than they had experienced in their previous home area. As Dave Clarke[29] of Blaen Plwyf has written, "this movement has continued with the discontent and pressures of urban life. The Rev. Williams would be pleased to know that today, in the uplands of Llanfair Clydogau and Llanddewi Brefi, even though some of the farms he knew as a boy are still in ruins, there is a thriving community of people living where he never thought to see people again".

Perhaps also, these incomers perceived that they could obtain more property for their money in an area which was in serious population and economic decline at this time. Whatever their intentions, these early incomers were often characterised by having little capital and had to find ways in which they could generate an income in an area in which paid employment was in short supply.

Many of those who arrived at this time, often initially lived in temporary accommodation such as a caravan. Records show that there were frequent debates within the parish council about their arrival. The spread of occupied caravans without planning permission and the alternative lifestyle of the newcomers were matters which prompted much discussion. Some of them moved to purchase empty and sometimes abandoned farmsteads. In the early 70's some of these changed hands for as little as £600, a building together with some land. Several medium sized small holdings on the uplands were sold for around £2,000. The new owners then spent a great deal of their own time and effort in repairing and renovating their new property. Hence the population decline was to some extent, arrested. One consequence of this was that the parish did not pass beyond the critical figure below which some of the upland roads would cease to be maintained, the Llanfair shop might have become uneconomic and other services would have declined.

This slow but steady inward migration has continued into the 1980's, and 90's, albeit against a background of fewer housing bargains to be had and with less emphasis upon the use of temporary accommodation by the incomers.

Sunday Schools

All the specific Sunday School buildings listed in Chapter Five, outlining the history of the 19th century, have long since ceased to operate. Those buildings mentioned in Llanddewi Brefi and Cellan can still be seen, though they are either in ruins or empty. Capel Mair's Maes Glas ceased being used in the early 1920's, became ruined and has now largely disappeared into a pile of stones.

The Gogoyan Sunday School just across the parish boundary in Llanddewi

Brefi, also ceased being used in the 20th century and today stands empty and boarded up as the picture of August 2008 shows below.

Gogoyan Sunday School

The building now known as Ysgoldy Fach stopped being used by the church in the 1970's. Minutes of the church report that on 26th May 1957, discussion took place about this building which was then called Ysgoldy'r Mynydd. It was stated that, "repairs would need to be taken immediately if the building was to be saved. Nothing had been done to it for many years". By November repair work was underway. In 1959, the Vicar spoke of the "summer services held at the Mountain Schoolroom and the good attendances". This was after the repairs initiated in 1957.

The church minutes of 1975 show discussion of the possible sale of Ysgoldy'r Mynydd which was described as a "dilapidated building located in an area where there were hardly any families remaining who came to the church". In 1976, when the sale was completed, it was described as being in danger of collapsing and of no further use as a mission hall. It has since been most successfully renovated and is used as a house.

Ysgoldy Fach (Mynydd) c 1976

Sunday School teachers from Capel Mair

Chapter Six 1900 to 2008

The church and the parish.

Minutes of the church from 1921 until 1951 show it operating several services each Sunday, plus a Sunday School. Attendances were sufficient to fund the salary of a minister. During the second half of the century, the number of people attending church services has continued to decline and the church is now operated as part of an area Ministry Team. Nevertheless weekly, largely bilingual services are still operating in 2008. Some of these changes can be seen from a consideration of the church minutes.

Key quotations from the Vestry minutes provide us with information about the position of the church within the community, the continuing decline in the population, the arrival of more English speaking residents and the impact of the Second World War. For instance:

- 1937, discussion about whether to hold an evening service. Concern that this "might tend to spoil the present comparatively good attendance at the present afternoon service and that the best course of action is not additional services, but more faithful attendance at the existing services". And that "the additional evening service might occasionally be held not in the parish church but in the Church Room in the uplands of Llanfair".
  This is Ysgoldy'r Mynydd;
- 1937, "the Vicar reminded those present that…members should do all in their power to encourage the attendance at services of people who were slack and indifferent";
- 1944 (Dec), decision to hold the annual Christmas Carol Concert in amalgamation with Capel Mair "during the war period";
- Dec 1945, decided that the Christmas Concert should be united with Capel Mair once more in order to support the Welcome Home Fund for returning service men, but that, "as in previous years, church and chapel to be responsible for their own tea". It was understood that the present arrangement was a temporary one.

Chapter Six
1900 to 2008

However in Dec. 1946 and 1947 the same arrangement was again made;
- 1955, "In order to cater for the spiritual needs of the many English people resident in the parish, it was decided to institute an English Service (for a trial period), on the second Sunday afternoon in each month". Reference to fund raising money to pay for a memorial lectern to commemorate service men killed in the war;"
- 1957, collection for Lampeter College Appeal. Also a plan to repair and beautify the church. Mrs Webb of Carmarthen had proceeded to install a stained glass window in the Sanctuary in memory of her parents, the Rev. and Mrs J.N. Evans. This was to a design prepared by the Celtic Studios, Prospect Place, Swansea, with the subject being the Supper at Emmaus;
- 1957, Porthcawl was the venue for the annual church outing;
- 1957, reported that Mrs Arthur of Gilfachieda Post Office intended presenting an oak table for the holding of church service books at the rear of the church;
- 1958, transfer of a disused font to Llangybi Church where no font currently existed;
- 1961, Mrs M. Jenkins, widow of the late Archdeacon of Merioneth, David Jenkins, a former native of Llanfair who is buried in the churchyard, had offered to install a Bishop's Sanctuary Chair in the Church. She had chosen a design submitted by the S.P.C.K. of Cardiff;
- 1973, there was a reference to the importance of legacies and bequests to help fund the church, "at a time when the population of the parish was dwindling";
- 1978, reference to the death of Mary Jones of Waunwen, Churchwarden, and the installation of a memorial window dedicated to both Mary and her husband;
- 1984, Aled Williams the current rector for the area was referred to as the new vicar, (since 30th March 1984).

Chapter Six   1900 to 2008

Tom Thomas[30] has written of the powerful position which the St Mary's Church took in pre war society. "Sunday was a sacred day in the true sense of the word. No cutting sticks, no noise, a day of rest. The church was not only a place of worship, it was also a social gathering. In fact the meeting outside the church very often lasted longer than the church service...As you entered the church, ladies occupied the pews on the left and the men to the right. There was some wonderful singing there. Funerals were well supported".

The parish graveyard

The graveyard, though on the church site, serves the whole of the parish. In view of the presence of a very old yew tree whose girth suggests it dates from the years 1200-1300 on the site, it is apparent that the graveyard too, is extremely old. There is a suggestion that it was in fact developed in two phases, with a very old foundation added to in more recent times by the addition of further land. The basis for this suggestion is a controversy which blew up in 1925 between the St Mary's Parish Council and the Ecclesiastical Commissioners, over what was the correct size of the graveyard, and who was responsible for it. After several letters had been written and careful scrutiny of the tithe apportionment map of 1844 and the earliest Ordnance Survey maps, it was declared that the site probably developed in two stages and that the local church was responsible for all the land. The best way in which to summarise what is believed to be the situation is to quote the Ecclesiastical Commissioners letter of 25th February 1925.

"The Rector (Rev. J. N. Evans), informs my Commissioners that when he became the incumbent in 1894, the portion of the burial ground to the north side of the church and entrance path, comprising about three quarters of an acre, contained only a few graves, all of which were of a comparatively recent date. He was informed by the Churchwardens and others that the portion in question had been added to the original churchyard about 60 years previously (that is about 1834), the donation being made by Lord Carrington who was the owner of the adjoining land and the Llanfair Estate. It was then enclosed with a boundary fence being erected about 30 years ago[31]".

The visual evidence on the site suggests that this statement is probably accurate, with a large slice of land around the yew tree lacking grave headstones, and hence probably very old, whilst the rest of the graveyard has many headstones.

Responsibility for maintaining the graveyard resides with the church and is an important obligation which is exercised for the whole of the parish. Historically this was undertaken by working parties of parishioners. More recently, parishioners have repaired the graveyard wall and cleared overgrown trees, whilst grass cutting is normally undertaken by a contractor.

Working party at Llanfair graveyard, early 20th century

Chapter Six   1900 to 2008

For anyone wanting detail of burials there are two sources. Firstly the St Mary's church record of all burials from 1748. This information is available in the National Library or via the church. Secondly a booklet listing details of all grave headstones, together with their inscriptions was prepared following research by a group of students from the University of Aberystwyth in 1994.

Visiting the graves of ancestors

There is a tradition within Wales which is well established in Llanfair, of an annual visit to place flowers on the grave of one's ancestors. This always occurs on Palm Sunday, the Sunday prior to Easter. It is known as "Flowering Sunday" or "Sul y Blodau". This particular day normally sees a steady flow of visitors to the graveyard with a number of former residents returning to honour their relatives.

Displays of remembrance within the church

The following are items within the church which add to the colour and significance of the inside of the building. They relate to individuals who have had important associations with Llanfair:

- Stained glass window: "To the Glory of God and in loving memory of Jonathan Evans, Vicar of this parish 1894-1935, and of Elizabeth, his devoted wife, respected and beloved by all who knew them";
- Stained glass window: "In grateful remembrance of James Thomas Jones, 1902-1971 and his wife Mary Jones, 1905-1977, loyal and generous churchwardens and parishioners";
- Inscription on a table: "In loving memory of Mary Griffiths, Lampeter 1929";

- Bishop's Chair, inscribed: " To the glory of God and in memory of David Jenkins (Archdeacon of Merioneth 1940-1952), given by his widow Mildred Jenkins";
- Bookcase inscription: "In loving memory of Dr. J.R.S. Webb of Carmarthen and his wife Mary, daughter of the Reverend J.N. Evans, former Rector of this parish, and his wife Elizabeth, presented by their children: Dr. John Webb, Mrs Elizabeth Stern, Mrs Eric Austin, September 1987";
- Table inscription: "To the glory of God and in loving memory of Ann Hodgkinson (1878-1957) a devoted mother and faithful member of this church".

Church Hall

The Church Hall building was constructed in the 20th century on land between the churchyard and the road. The history of its inception, construction, management and uses over time, can be gathered together from sources such as the church minutes, Llanfair Parish Council minutes and minutes of the Village Hall Committee.

The Annual Vestry meeting of the church, records that Joseph Evans of Llanfair Fawr, gave the land on which the Hall stands. Joseph was the brother of the vicar, the Reverend Jonathan Evans. In 1933, the same minutes report that his son Gwyn was mainly responsible for raising £1,370 to build the Hall, and that he took an active part in the actual building work. In 1969 Gwyn gave more land to be added within the curtilage of the building so that a toilet block could be built. The records show that he was a stalwart of both the church and the parish. He served as a churchwarden continuously for 45 years and, already a Justice of the Peace, he was awarded the O.B.E. in 1968. In 1939 there is a reference to the need to deal with the level of debt of £34 on the Church Hall by a "canvass of the church people, the parish and other sympathisers to solicit contributions for the clearing of the debt". Mr Gwyn Evans and Mr David Jones, Churchwardens were to lead the canvass. In 1940 there was still concern with the deficit of the Church Hall, which then stood at £19.1s.5d.

Gwyn Evans receiving a retirement gift from the Rev. Aled Williams

The Hall was requisitioned during the Second World War by the Ministry of Food and released in 1945, as a result, "we would be able in future to renew normal activities and social functions". There was a Hall piano which had been kept in excellent condition by Miss Jones of Parcneuadd during the war period.

In 1946 there was a request to the church from the newly formed branch of Urdd Gobaith Cymru to use the Church Hall. It was agreed they could hire the kitchenette area for 1 shilling per night. The Urdd was to be responsible for coal and lights. The Easter 1950 church minutes record that Gwyn Evans "brought forward the question of installing the church and hall with electric light", since mains electricity had recently arrived in the lowland part of the parish. After a deferment to allow for more consideration, it was decided to proceed on 30th April. Following a tendering process, a contract for the work was later given to Mr Williams of Lampeter and the scheme completed to fit in with the October Harvest Festival of 1950.

In 1965 it was reported that when a sewerage scheme was undertaken in the village, it was important to see that the Church Hall was connected and water then made available for use.

In 1968 a church meeting approved the plan for connection of the Church Hall to the new village sewerage system.

In 1969, whilst plastering work was being carried out in the church, religious services were temporarily moved to the Church Hall. Other work being undertaken included treatment of timber and the fixing of electric radiant heaters. Planning permission for the erection of a toilet block at the Church Hall was also received during that year. In 1971 it was reported that much had been spent on the construction of the new toilet block at the Hall, including £268.18s.4d from the Deposit Account. Mains water supply had also been installed. In 1977 the minutes show discussions took place with regard to the high cost of painting the Church Hall, and in 1984 there was a decision taken to install new electric convector heaters. In 1985 it was decided to publicise the availability of the building for public hire and Tommy Williams was asked to erect a notice board on the churchyard wall.

The minutes of the Llanfair Community Council show the Hall being used for its meetings and in 1994, Councillors decided to give a grant of £650 to help fund a renovation scheme for the building.

A major change occurred on 16 March 2001 when a village trust was established to run the Hall in the interests of the parish, in agreement with St David's Diocese, the owners of the Hall. The four signatories of the Agreement were David Jones, Ian Evans, Arwyn Davies and Elizabeth Mercer. From the beginning, the focus was upon its development as a meeting place and social centre. Over the years since then, a wide range of activities have taken place within the Hall each year. In the past 12 months, those actions which have taken place include carol singing; games night; bingo; cawl and whist; local history exhibition; village fete; twmpath and a barbecue. From the beginning, steps were taken to renovate and improve the fabric of the Hall. Some of these involved members of the parish undertaking work such as removal of the stage. In addition, after successful fund raising among residents along with applications for grant funding, other work was undertaken. This included the installation of central heating and improvements to the kitchen. In 2006 the toilets were renovated and a new electrical system was installed, again following fund raising and applications for grant aid. Money came from Llanfair Community Council, Ceredigion County Council and the Wales Council for Voluntary Access Actions. In May 2008 the asbestos roof tiles were replaced by Welsh slates. In a very imaginative action, the slates used were purchased from a company in Rawtenstall, Lancashire, having previously been used on the roof of a Sunday School in that area. Financing the roof was a major task which involved a successful bid to Ceredigion Council for £8,050 and to the National Lottery for £5,000, along with a whole range of fund raising activities in the parish to augment this amount. All of the successful applications for funding to outside bodies were drafted and submitted by the then Secretary of the Village Hall Committee, Elizabeth Mercer of Gelli Ddyfod.

Renovating the Village Hall roof, May 2008 : contractors are Llanfair residents Laurence and Linda Quelch (middle of photograph) with Alan Dickson (to the left)

Chapter Six   1900 to 2008

Maintaining the church and graveyard

The minutes of the Annual Vestry meeting show that maintaining the fabric of the building was an important consideration, as was the maintenance of the graveyard which is for both church and chapel. For instance:

- 1936, painting and varnishing the whole church, approved a quotation for this from Mr. A Price of Lampeter of £25;
- 1937, it was agreed to purchase two more lamps for the better lighting of the church;
- January 1957, "The electricity authority had installed 3 electric Champion Heaters for the members to test their efficiency (and without obligation to purchase). Their permanent purchase was later confirmed, plus a fourth";
- 1960, a plan to "undertake a heavy programme of repairs needed on the fabric of the church";
- 1961, report of a successful whist drive to raise money and a collaborative effort to cut the grass within the church yard. Concern expressed at the poor condition of the church roof. At a further meeting it was reported that the roofing contractor had failed to slate the defective section of the roof due to the fact that "his assistant was indisposed";
- 1963, it was reported that the Area Superintendent of the War Graves Commission on a recent visit, had complimented the Parish on the maintenance of the churchyard;
- 1963, a major programme of church restoration had been undertaken. This included: re roofing much of the church; erecting new copings; insertion of lead soakings and flashings, new guttering and downpipes; re pointing of the west end and other elevations; laying of new concrete paths around the church and Hall. The craftsman in charge was Mr. T. J. Williams of Llwyngog "who had done an excellent job". To fund this heavy expense would

necessitate an appeal for funds. The appeal generated £1,673.10s.6d from individual subscriptions, this included people drawn from a wide area. Some 183 personal or family donations were made from as far afield as Calgary, Alberta, Canada, London, Devon, Wolverhampton and Hampshire, though the bulk of the money received came from local residents. Recording his thanks for the donations made the Rev. Mathias wrote, "I am convinced that although the parish of Llanfair has lost many of its inhabitants because of rural depopulation, the church is remembered and loved by a wide circle of friends living today far beyond its Parish boundaries. It is the centre of their childhood memories and its churchyard is the resting place of their loved ones" [32]. The funding generated came from a whole range of people and families. There was a high level of involvement of members of Capel Mair as well as members of the Church;

- 1966, an appeal to church members to assist with the rebuilding of the churchyard boundary fence;
- 1971, a tender for £202 from Jones brothers of Lampeter to decorate the church was accepted.

The Llanfair and Cellan Young Farmers Club (YFC)

The Llanfair and Cellan Young Farmers Club was formed on 12th October 1942 at a meeting held at Cellan Church Hall. At the outset, one of its aims was to work in association with the Urdd. At the inaugural meeting, Councillor Gwyn Evans of Llanfair Fawr was appointed President, with Chairman Mr D.T. Davies of Castell, Secretary, Miss Nancy Thomas of Blaenplwyf and Club Leader, Mr W. R. Lloyd Jones of Llanfair Fach. Regular meetings were planned and took place, mainly during the winter months and often on a weekly basis, with visiting speakers and events such as public speaking competitions. Such was the popularity of the organisation that at its fourth annual meeting in 1945 there was an attendance of 40 people. Talks took place on such topics as "electricity on the farm", the Milk Marketing Board and milk production, science in wartime, animal husbandry, "livestock policy of the Ministry", plant breeding, farm accidents, home carpentry for boys along with needlework and cookery for girls.

Llanfair-Cellan Y.F.C.
1945—46.

OFFICIALS:

President—Gwyn Evans, C.C., Llanfair-fawr
Club Leader—John James, Llwynbedw
Chairman—Sylvan Griffiths, Pentre
Vice-Chairman—Pat Evans, Fisher's Arms
Treasurer—Betty Jones, Pontfaen
Secretary—John Davies, Brynmeuog
Press Reporter—Glenys Evans, Brynawel
Librarian—Tilly Jones, Glanteify

D. R. Evans & Co., Bridge Press, Lampeter.

Detail of the membership for the Young Farmers Club in the year 1945-1946

Programme.

1945
- Sept. 24 — Business Meeting
- Oct. 1 — J. A. George, Esq., Planning a County Rally
- Oct. 5 — Social Evening
- Oct. 9 — Elfyn Owen, Esq., N.D.A., N.D.D. Fireside Chat
- Oct. 15 — F. Gregg, Esq. Electricity on the Farm
- Oct. 22 — W. Evans, Esq. Winter Feeding
- Oct. 29 — W. G. Hughes, Esq. Ancient Customs
- Nov. 5 — — Davies, Esq., (Veterinary Surgeon) Treatment of minor ailments in cattle
- Nov. 12 — D. Egryn Jones, Esq. Machinery Films
- Nov. 19 — D. J. Morgan, Esq. Atgofion Bore Oes
- Nov. 26 — Agri. B Visitors—Llanwnen Y.F.C.
- Dec. 3 — Mrs. Bowen Bacon Curing
- Dec. 10 — I. G. Williams, Esq. Grading of Fat Stock
- Dec. 17 — — Rees, Esq., Llwyncelyn Brush Making
- Dec. 24 — Noson Lawen

1946
- Jan. 7 — Watcyn Williams, Esq. Grassland Management
- Jan. 14 — Mrs. James Own Topic
- Jan. 21 — Public Speaking
- Jan. 28 — County Poultry Advisor Poultry Judging and Trussing
- Feb. 4 — Miss Jane Davies Films
- Feb. 11 — Agri. B. Contest Guests—Caio & Llancrwys Y.F.C.
- Feb. 18 — Brains Trust
- Feb. 25 — R. L. Jones, Esq. Farm Planning
- Mar. 4 — President's Open Night
- Mar. 11 — Mrs. Bowen Preserves and Bottling
- Mar. 18 — Club Leader's Open Night
- Mar. 25 — Winding-up Social

Detail of the programme for the Young Farmers Club in the year 1945-1946

Chapter Six   1900 to 2008

Llanfair achieved prominence in 1943 when it held a Semi Rally (covering a wide geographical area) of the YFC. John Davies[33] of Bryn Castell, has spoken to me of the importance of the YFC at this time.

The geographical location for meetings shifted in November 1948 to Llanfair, where the Church Hall became the venue. This arrangement is shown as continuing through until the last minuted meeting of 20th March 1950.

The reasons for the ending of the YFC are unknown. The following may constitute influences:

- By 1950, the numbers of people attending had dropped to 12-14;
- A rival YFC, serving Cellan was set up called Cellan "B" Young Farmers Club. In January of 1950 Jenkin Jones, Organising Secretary, asked on behalf of Cellan "B" if the Llanfair and Cellan YFC would agree to the dropping of the word Cellan from its title to reduce confusion. However, this suggestion was not supported.
- Changes in the pattern of society and the economy. The worst aspects of the period of wartime austerity was coming to an end and there were more opportunities emerging for social activities outside the YFC.

Forestry Commission

In the 20th Century, the formal planting of new forests in the Llanfair area took place by the Forestry Commission. The Commission was established by an Act of Parliament in 1919, with the aim of promoting the interests of forestry, the development of afforestation and the production of timber in England, Wales and Scotland. The organisation appeared in the parish after the Second World War, purchasing upland farms where the buildings had been abandoned and farming was difficult and uneconomic. Evan Davies,[34] who ran the Llanfair Shop in the 1960's and some of the 1970's, and before that farmed on the Llanfair uplands, has helped identify some of the forestry

Chapter Six   1900 to 2008

---

developments. In 1950 he owned Esgair Fraith (a ruined building plus 70 acres), at a height of about 1200 feet on the Cardiganshire-Carmarthenshire boundary, which he farmed with sheep. In about 1953/4 he, along with other farmers operating at this altitude, sold his land to the Forestry Commission for £10 per acre. Planting of trees then began in about 1955. Today, a large swathe of the mountainside is covered with conifers which are managed for the production of timber. A number of farm units which were shown on the 1906 Ordnance Survey map and the 1910 Valuation Survey, have disappeared from view, having been swallowed up by the plantations. Walking along some of the forest tracks today leads to a number of ruined farm buildings.

Forestry Commission plantations on the hills above Llanfair

Longwood

A major project under the auspices of Cydcoed, saw a local community group receive funding under the European Union's Objective 1, for a scheme to develop for community use, the Longwood area which lies

Chapter Six

1900 to 2008

between Llanfair and Llangybi. The land is owned by the National Assembly and is an area of ancient, semi natural woodland with a mixture of broadleaf

Typical upland land use above Llanfair : sheep and forestry

and conifer plantations. It lies close to a line of ancient Bronze Hill forts.

In May 2008, the Longwood Community Group held an official opening of the site attended by Ceredigion Assembly Member Elin Jones. The plan is to develop bridleways, access points, parking and information areas. The grant awarded to support the Longwood development totalled £195,863.

Shops

Until the middle years of the 20th century, small retail outlets existed at Glan Rhyd selling tea and sugar, and at Cwrt y Cylchau. There was also a sales point for paraffin at a house in the centre of the village called Ty Lôn, now demolished and removed. The main shop serving the parish has continued, as it had in the 19th century, to be that located at Llanfair Bridge. Evan Davies[35] recalls installing petrol tanks and pumps (National Benzol), the arrival at Llanfair Bridge of mains water around 1960 and then later, mains sewerage for houses close by. The petrol pumps have now been

Chapter Six   1900 to 2008

removed. Evan also remembers visits to the parish of itinerant Breton onion sellers and salesmen from India calling at houses to try to sell their goods.

Llanfair Shop showing petrol pumps which have since been removed

Snippets of news from Llanfair

- January 1975, discussion about local government reorganisation. "Passed that if there was to be a reorganisation, Cellan, Llanfair, Llangybi and Betws should get together". In October 1975, a decision was taken that any reorganisation should be with Cellan (Parish Council minutes).
- In June 1977, all village children were presented with a mug to commemorate the Queen's Silver Jubilee at a function held on 6th June. It was described as a great success. The cost was 35p each. (Parish Council minutes).

Chapter Six   1900 to 2008

- 1978, decision taken to construct a bus shelter at a cost of £380. By 1979, this was revised to £425. It was to be constructed on land leased from Ceredigion Council. However, there was difficulty in persuading the contractor to do the work and as a result, it was not proceeded with at this time. A development in 1987 saw land given to the County Council by Gwyn Evans of Maes Gwyn, on condition that the shelter was built of stone. Work started in 1988. The tender price was £1,619. (Parish Council minutes).

- 1977-9, much discussion took place about abandoned scrap cars on various properties. Various discussions about inhabited caravans and how to deal with the issue. (Parish Council minutes).

- 7th May 1995, VE celebrations held. All children given a £2 coin. Carnival and sports day held at Cellan. Tea and sandwiches provided. At Llanfair a barbecue was held and twmpath with Erwyd Howells. A national 2 minute silence was held during the twmpath.(Parish Council minutes).

- In July 1968, the Cambrian News carried a report and photograph of Llanfair residents gathered around a "mysterious object" which descended by parachute onto land at Penlan. The object turned out to be a gamma ray telescope belonging to Bristol University which had been launched from RAF Cardington to try to detect gamma rays from outer space. (Cambrian News).

- In June 2008, British Telecom began a public consultation about the possible withdrawal of thousands of telephone boxes across the UK, one of which is that located at Pont Glanrhyd.

Chapter Six   1900 to 2008

Telephone box at Pont Glanrhyd

Capel Mair

Capel Mair has continued to operate successfully throughout this period. It remains an important centre of religious worship in the parish, though, like St Mary's, with smaller congregations. Weekly services operated until 1988 when the pattern changed to once monthly. This switch was at the time of the retirement of the Rev. D. Morlais Jones, the last of a long line of full time ministers of the chapel. From this date, services have been led by visiting ministers.

Official members of Capel Mair totalled 103 in 1942, 92 in 1947 and 72 in 1957. The decline closely matched the reduction in inhabitants within the parish. By 1980 there were 30 members, 1990 some 27, whilst in the period 2005-7 there were 24.

As a record of important developmental events of the 20th century, in 1951 the chapel vestry was built and some renovation work was carried out on the building at this time. In the same year new furniture was donated by various members. 1958 marks the date when electricity was first installed.

Glanrhyd family wedding at Capel Mair

The Royal Commission on the Historic and Ancient Monuments of Wales lists the Capel Mair building as having historical significance.

The chapel contains an impressive Bardic Chair which was won by the Rev. J. Neddfryn Davies, who was a minister there from 1894-1901. He married a chapel member, Ann Griffiths of Blaencwm and later, after joining the Church in Wales, became vicar of Llandyfaelog in Carmarthenshire. Upon his death his wife returned to live with her brother at Pentre and donated the Bardic Chair for use in the chapel pulpit.

A celebratory event for the chapel's 175th anniversary was held in October 2000 with a dinner at Tregaron. The guest speaker was the Rev. W.J. Gruffydd. A Cymanfa Ganu (Singing Festival), was held at Capel Mair at which the President was Emyr Davies of Cardiff.

Chapter Six 1900 to 2008

SWYDDOGION, &c., CAPEL MAIR.

Yn eistedd (o'r chwith): Mri. Rees George, Rees Lewis, Parch. J. D. Jones, Mri. Joshua Davies, John Jones (Pedwar Diacon a'r Gweinidog).
Yn sefyll (o'r chwith): Miss M. Lloyd (Organyddes), Mrs. J. D. Jones, Mri. David Griffiths (Diacon, Trysorydd, a Arweinydd y Canu), Daniel Evans (Ysgrifenydd), Miss M. Griffiths (Organyddes).

Officials of Capel Mair, early in the 20th century

Members of Capel Mair, 1988

216

Chapter Six   1900 to 2008

Llanfair History Exhibition: August 2008

Following a suggestion to the Village Hall Committee early in 2008 by Laura Wood, it was agreed to hold an exhibition on the history of the parish of Llanfair. This took place from 9th -16th August in the Village Hall. For the months leading up to the date, a group of about 10 local residents worked hard to read and research the history of Llanfair and to gather together examples of agricultural implements and examples of household life from the late 19th and early 20th centuries. For some, this involved visits to the National Library, National Archives, Ceredigion Archives and Ceredigion Museum in order to obtain copies of maps and significant legal documents. The exhibition was an outstanding success, with a good attendance of visitors each day and many positive comments made in the visitors book.

Historic exhibits within the Village Hall, including clothing from Blaen Cwm and Llanfair Fach.

Carts from Llanfair Fach, outside the Village Hall

Some Llanfair residents

The Jones Ladies of Waunwen (Maria, Hetty and Liza)

Tom Thomas[36] has described how the three ladies were held in great esteem within the parish in the 1920's and 1930's. "When you saw the Waunwen ladies driven to church on a Sunday in their pony and trap-they went to Llanddewi, but I don't know why- they were stately and dignified and one couldn't help standing aside and raising one's cap. They were the people to go to when you wanted advice which they freely gave. One had to admit that they were better informed than us, and very influential. They certainly didn't regard us as being inferior-they treated us as equals and we thought a lot of them."

James Thomas Jones and his wife Mary, of Waunwen

Mr and Mrs Jones were well known Llanfair residents and parishioners. They were churchwardens of St Mary's and there is a stained glass window in their remembrance in the church. James lived 1902-71 and Mary 1905-77.

The Thomas's of Llanfair Fach and Llanfair House

Chapter Six   1900 to 2008

Mary Thomas (1841 -1916)) and her daughters, Margaret Anne Thomas (1880-1952), Rachel (1873-1955) and Mary (1883-1966). These photographs were taken in about 1890 and 1910 and show Mary Thomas and her daughters. In 1881, when the head of the family, William Thomas was still alive, they lived and farmed at Llanfair Fach.

Conclusion.

Llanfair has a modern written history of almost 500 years, and a traceable history of about 2000 years. The account within this book has sought to record as much of this history as possible for the benefit not only for those present and past residents who love, respect and cherish the parish, but also for visitors and those with an interest in local history.

Vicars of St Mary's (showing one or more years when the incumbent was in post, a discontinuous and incomplete record):

1535 Thomas Lloyd (with Llanddewi Collegiate Church);

1707 Daniel Rowland;

1755-73 Rees Thomas;

1775 T. Probert;

1775-79 Rice Williams;

1782 Evan Williams;

1792-1842 David Williams;

1842-1859 Morgan Williams;

1860-1894 William Evans;

1894- Jonathan Evans;

1938- D.A. Jenkins;

1941- Joshua Davies;

1942- J.W. Hughes;

1955- J. M. Mathias;

1984- continuing, Aled Williams (canon: oversight of group of churches working collaboratively, called Bro Teifi Sarn Helen).

Ministers of Capel Mair:

1825-52, Rev. David Stephens;

1852-92, Rev. Thomas Thomas;

1894-1901 Rev. J. Neddfyn Davies;

1902-1910 Rev. T. Eli Evans;

1912-1929 Rev. J.D. Jones;

1930-1938 Rev. W. Aneurin Jenkins;

1940-1947 Rev. D. Morlais Jones, B.A.;

1948-1956 Rev. R. Anthony Davies;

1958-1974 Rev. D.D.R. Phillips;

1975-1976 Rev. H.T. Samuel;

1983-1988 Rev. D. Morlais Jones, B.A.;

1988- visiting ministers, with monthly services.

Elders of Capel Mair:

Elders in 1940: Joshua Davies, Haulfre;
D. W. Griffiths, Pentre;
Timothy George, Llwynowen;
Evan Evans, Esger maen;
Daniel Evans, Glanrhyd,

Elders in 1947: D. W. Griffiths, Pentre;
Timothy George, Llwynowen;
Joseph Rees, Is-coed;
David Evans, Nantymedd;
David Lewis, Cefnfoelallt;
W. R. Lloyd Jones, Llanfair Fach.

Elders in 1973: Daniel Lewis, Vaeliog Villa;
W.R. Lloyd Jones, Llanfair Fach;
Glyn Evans, Esger maen;
Ian Evans, Esger maen.

Elders in 1981: W.R. Lloyd Jones, Llanfair Fach;
H. T. Davies, Hafod, Tregaron;
Ian Evans, Esger maen;
Tommy Roberts, Fronhaul.

Elders in 1984: H.T. Davies, Hafod, Tregaron;
Ian Evans, Esger maen;
Tommy Roberts, Bronhaul;
Iris Quan, Blaencwm.

High Sheriffs of Cardiganshire from Plas Llanfair:

1551- David ap Evan Llwyd Fychan, Esq;

1557- David ap Evan Llwyd Fychan, Esq.;

1570- David ap Evan Lloyd Fychan, Esq.;

1578- Jenkin Lloyd, Esq;

1591- Jenkin Lloyd, Esq;

1603- John Lloyd, Esq;

1622- Walter Lloyd, Esq;

1656- Thomas Lloyd, Esq;

1674- Thomas Johnes, Esq;

1705- Thomas Johnes, Esq.

Members of Parliament from Plas Llanfair or Hafod:

1640-3   - Walter Lloyd (Cardiganshire);

1713-4   - Thomas Johnes (the 1st Thomas Johnes of Hafod) (Cardiganshire);

1774-80 - Thomas Johnes (Cardigan Boroughs);

1802-6   - Thomas Johnes (Cardiganshire and later, Radnor).

References

Chapter One: Introduction

1. Jonathan Evans, November 30th 1909 in Cardiganshire Antiquarian Society.
2. Trevor Lewis: Archaeological Investigations in the vicinity of Llanddewi Brefi and Llanfair Clydogau, Transactions of the Cardiganshire Antiquarian Society, 1927.
3. David Austin: "Excavations and Survey at Bryn Cysegrfan, Llanfair Clydogau, 1979, in Medieval Archaeology 32, 1988 p 130-165.
4. Pevsner Architectural Guides: "Carmarthenshire and Ceredigion" 2006.
5. Valor Ecclesiasticus, survey for Henry VIII 1535.
6. Lewis, "A topographical dictionary of Cardiganshire" 1825.
7. Cardiganshire County History, volume 1, 1994.
8. Royal Commission on the Ancient and Historical Monuments of Wales, Aberystwyth.
9. Llanfair Clydogau Church Font, in Cardiganshire Antiquarian Society 1913, Vol 1, No 3.
10. Francis Jones: "Cardiganshire Homes and Families", 2004.
11. Freeholders list for Cardiganshire, from Historical Society of West Wales, Vol III, 1913.
12. Elizabeth Inglis-Jones: "Peacocks in Paradise", 1990 reprint.
13. Samuel Rush Meyrick: "The History of Cardiganshire", first published 1810, reprint 2000.
14. Unpublished paper on Llanfair mining by Thomas Griffiths of Blaen Cwm, c1888/90. In the possession of his daughter Iris Quan of Blaen Cwm

Chapter Two: 1500-1599

1. Valor Ecclesiasticus, op. cit..
2. Glanmor Williams: " The Welsh Church from Conquest to Reformation" 1962.
3. Lewis Dwnn: "Heraldic Visitation of the Counties of Carmarthen, Pembroke and Cardigan, dated 1586; published in 1846 by S. R. Meyrick.
4. Lucy Theakston and John Davies, quote in "Some family records and pedigrees...." 1913
5. Will of David ap Jevons, National Library of Wales (NLW).
6. Crosswood manuscript, NLW

Chapter Three: 1600-1699

1. Exchequer proceedings concerning Wales, Tempore James I, compiled by T.I. Jones, 1955.
2. Exchequer proceedings concerning Wales, Tempore James I, compiled by T. I. Jones, 1955.
3. Cwrtmawr deed, 1613 manuscript, NLW.
4. Various extracts of Walter Lloyd's biography.
5. Letters from Cardigan County Committee to the Committee for Compoundery, London, 1646, 1650.
6. Bronwydd manuscript of 1669 re marriage of Thomas Jones of
7. Dolaucothi to the daughter of Walter Lloyd of Llanvair (note the spelling of Jones, not Johnes), NLW.
8. Various Llanfair wills, manuscripts NLW.
9. Will of Walter Lloyd of Olmarch, 1691, manuscript NLW.
10. Edward Lhwyd: "Letters of Edward Lhwyd, 1697, re published by Cambrian Archaeological Association 1909.

11. Tom Thomas, talk "Llanfair before the War", with written notes (2006) and subsequent conversation summer 2008.

Chapter Four: 1700-1799

1. St David's Diocese Manuscript, NLW.
2. Erasmus Saunders: " A view of the state of religion in the Diocese of St David's, about the beginning of the 18th Century, 1721.
3. David Lloyd Davies, unpublished Lampeter University thesis on St David's diocese..
4. St David's Diocese manuscript, NLW.
5. St Mary's Vestry minutes, NLW.
6. George Eyre Evans: "Cardiganshire" 1903 in Archaeologica Cambrensis.
7. Conversation with Iris Quan of Blaen Cwm, summer 2008.
8. Conversation with Gwyneth Jones of Noyadd, summer 2008.
9. A.G. Bradley: "Highways and Byways in South Wales" 1903.
10. Thomas Johnes' will of 1733, Hafod papers, Ceredigion Archives.
11. Wedding agreement of Thomas Johnes, 1746, Hafod papers, Ceredigion Archives.
12. Elizabeth Inglis Jones, Peacocks in Paradise, op. Cit..
13. G. W. Hall "Metal Mines of Southern Wales" 1993, quotes W. L. Lewis.
14. Docaucothi papers, NLW.
15. Thomas Griffiths, op. cit..
16. Davies in History of Cardiganshire Vol 3, section on the poor law.
17. W. J. Lewis: "Labour in Mid Cardiganshire in the early 19th century. Cardiganshire Antiquarian Society 1963.
18. Crime and Punishment records, NLW.
19. Llanfair freeholders & leaseholders, 1760, from Historical Society of West Wales, Vol 3 1913.

20. Llanfair and Llanddewi Brefi Estates, T. Lewis 1791, NLW.

Chapter Five: 1800-1899

1. Fenton, "Tours of Wales" 1804-13, Cambrian Archaeological Association, reprint 1913.
2. S.R. Merrick, quoted in Chapter 1.
3. Barber: "A Tour of South Wales" 1803.
4. B. H. Malkin "The scenery, antiquities and biography of S Wales" 1803, pub. 1804.
5. Nanteos manuscript, 1817, NLW.
6. W. J. Lewis "Labour in Mid Cardiganshire in the early 19th century", Cardigan Antiquarian Society 1963.
7. St David's Diocese manuscript, NLW.
8. Ieuan Gywnedd Jones: " People's Heath in mid Victorian Wales", Transactions of the Honorable Society of Cymmrodorion, 1984.
9. Ieuan Gwynedd Jones: "The elections of 1865 and 1868", Trans of the Hon. Soc. Of Cymmrodorion, 1964.
10. Rev David Williams: "Y Wladfa Fach Fynyddig", 1963.
11. R. Burt, et al: "The Mines of Cardiganshire 1845-1913".
12. G. W. Hall "Metal Mines of Southern Wales", 1993.
13. Lewis, Topographical Dictionary of Wales, 1833.
14. Simon Timberlake, Bryn Cysegrfan: Llanfair Clydogau Leat, Archeology in Wales, 42, 2002.
15. David Austin , op. cit...
16. Arwyn Evans, of Llanfair Fawr conversation of August 2008.
17. Lewis, op. cit..
18. Will held by NLW.
19. Beti Davies of Bryn Castell, conversation of September 2008.
20. The Welshman, June 1859.

21. Reports of the Commissioners to enquire concerning charities relating to the County of Cardigan 1819-1837, document in Lampeter University Library.
22. Article by Dan and Aerwen Griffiths in Clonc publication of 2002.
23. The Reports of the Commissioners appointed to enquire into the state of education in Wales, 1847.
24. Saunders Lewis, quoted by Gwyneth Tyson Robers, 1998 in "The Language of the Blue Books".
25. The Religious Census of Returns relating to Wales, Vol 1 South Wales, 1851.
26. Friedrich Engels: "The Condition of the Working Class in England", 1844.
27. Llanfair School Board minutes, Ceredigion Archives.
28. "History of Education in Ceredigion", Ceredigion County Council, web site.
29. Llanfair School Log Book, Ceredigion Archives.
30. W. Gareth Evans commenting on Aberdare Report in Ceredigion Antiquarian Society, Vol IX 1982.
31. Llanfair School Board minutes, Ceredigion Archives.
32. Biographical details from NLW.
33. Biographical details from NLW.
34. Rev. J.N. Evans, statement attached to St Mary's Church registers, NLW.
35. St David's Diocese manuscript, NLW.
36. Capel Mair: "Cyfrol y jiwbili" 1926.
37. Bert Rawlins: "The parish churches and non conformist chapels of Wales" 1987.
38. Matthew Cragoe: "Conscience or Coercion" in "Culture, Politics and national identity in Wales", 2004.
39. Tithe detail, NLW.
40. Religious Census of 1851, op. cit...

41. Morgan Williams detail is cited in the text: taken from National Archives, St. David's Diocese manuscripts NLW, parish records at NLW, Ceredigion Archives, Lampeter University Library, newspapers.
42. Queens Bench London, National Archives.
43. Writ: St David's Diocesan papers, NLW.
44. Sequestration papers, St David's Diocesan papers, NLW.
45. St David's Diocesan papers, NLW.
46. Minutes of Cardiganshire Quarter Sessions, Ceredigion Archives.
47. Minutes of Cardiganshire Quarters Sessions, Ceredigion Archives.
48. Carmarthen Journal, July 1859.
49. St David's Diocese manuscript, NLW.
50. St David's Diocese, Ecclesiastical Commission papers, NLW.
51. Carmarthen Journal, July 1859.
52. Carmarthen Journal, May 1860.
53. Document re W. Jones, NLW.
54. Archaeologica Cambrensis p 310, 1861.
55. St David's Diocesan papers, NLW.
56. Kelly's Directory, South Wales 1895.
57. Horsfall Turner: "Wanderings in Cardiganshire", undated.
58. Royal Commission on Land in Wales, etc 25 April, 1894.
59. .Capel Mair: "Cyfrol y Jiwbili", 1926.

Chapter Six: 1900-2008

1. A.G. Bradley: "Highways and Byways in South Wales" 1903.
2. School Board Minutes, op. cit..
3. Log Book, op. cit..
4. School Board minutes, op. cit..
5. Beti Davies conversation, op. cit..
6. Tom Thomas, op. cit..

7. Valuation Office Survey, 1910-15, National Archives.
8. Kelly's Directory, 1910.
9. An Assessment for the Relief of the Poor of Llanfair Clydogau" 1919, in Lampeter University Library.
10. Joseph Jenkins, in "Cerddi, Cerncogh by John Jenkins, 1938 publication.
11. Llanfair Parish Council Minutes, NLW.
12. Ian Evans, Esgairmaen conversation of summer 2008.
13. Bethan Phillips: "The Lovers Graves" 2007.
14. Will of William Jones, NLW.
15. Tom Thomas, op. cit..
16. Johnny Williams conversation, August 2008.
17. Bleddyn Williams conversation, August 2008.
18. St David's Diocesan papers, NLW.
19. Taylor-Lloyd: " 3rd Cardiganshire Battalion Home Guard" 1947.
20. 1941/3 Government Farm Survey, National Archives.
21. Welsh History Review, Dec. 2007, R.J. Moore-Colyer.
22. Evan Davies, conversation of July 2008.
23. Tom Thomas, op. cit..
24. Welsh Agricultural Land Sub Committee, quoted by E.G.Bowen: "Rural Wales" in "Great Britain Geographical Essays" by J. Mitchell, 1962
25. Dave Clarke, Blaen Plwyf : unpublished Lampeter University dissertation: " Aspects of the Landscape of the Nant Clywedog Uchaf Valley", 1995.
26. Vestry minutes of St Mary's.
27. Tom Thomas, op.cit..
28. St. David's Diocesan papers, NLW.
29. Restoration Appeal Document, Lent, 1965, St Mary's Church.
30. John Davies, conversation of September 2008.
31. Evan Davies, op. cit..

32. Evan Davies, op.cit..
33. Tom Thomas, op cit..